To Bill and Vonette Bright

for your example, inspiration and partnership in working toward closure of the Great Commission in our generation

ACKNOWLEDGMENTS

THE AUTHOR of Proverbs wrote, "Withhold not good from them to whom it is due, when it is in the power of thine hand to do it" (Prov. 3:27, KJV). In the spirit of this timely proverb I wish to use the power of my pen to acknowledge with gratitude those who have given many extra hours of sacrificial labor to prepare this manuscript for publication.

Very special thanks goes to Linda Thede who completely re-typed the manuscript several times and also devoted many hours in preparing the substantive index that appears at the end of the book. To Marie Reyes I say thank you for preparing the very first draft of *The Jericho Hour,* and to Faustino Ruivivar I gratefully acknowledge your meticulous editorial gifts. To my wife, Dee, I thank you for putting up with my many long nights of extra work while the manuscript was being finalized. To Dick Koeth, a gifted consultant to our ministry, I express special thanks for suggesting to me during the early days of the fall of communism in Eastern Europe that the church was now entering the Jericho hour. From that conversation emerged this book and its title. And to Tommie Femrite, a committed personal intercessor, special thanks for an obedient "word" in a prayer time that prompted me to add the last chapter to this book.

Special acknowledgment also goes to our ten thousand full-time staff and devoted field volunteers in the ministry of Every Home for Christ. They physically take a message of the gospel of Jesus Christ to more than 350,000 new families every week, resulting in over 500,000 annual decision cards being received for follow-up. May this book help mobilize the prayer and financial support each of these so desperately needs to help finish the task of world evangelization in our generation. ⧗

CONTENTS

THE WONDER years of world evangelization are here! Some missiologists and church-growth experts believe it is quite possible that more souls could come to Christ between now and the end of this century than in all of recorded church history. This book is about that harvest and how an emerging understanding of strategic-level "warfare prayer" followed by unprecedented united evangelism strategies is making it possible.

Of course, implicit in any discussion of warfare is that one side will ultimately win. Further, the side that gains the victory will claim the spoils. For believers the spoils of victory are the souls of men and women — Satan's most cherished possession. Indeed, in all of our talk of spiritual warfare we must not forget this essential fact.

As David Bryant, president of Concerts of Prayer International, explains, "If our warfare doesn't result in the fulfillment of the Great Commission, it hasn't succeeded."[1]

Edgardo Silvoso, the Argentine missions strategist, adds: "We must measure all our results of spiritual warfare in how much we loot the enemy's camp."[2]

According to both Bryant's and Silvoso's analyses, the church has been making encouraging headway in its warfare for the nations. At the start of this decade, missions researchers estimated that the church was growing by approximately seventy thousand new Christians per day. Now that figure may well exceed a hundred thousand daily. Some missiologists believe that number could grow significantly in the immediate days ahead as barriers hindering the spread of the gospel continue to fall. I believe the church has entered the wonder years of world evangelization.

On the pages that follow, I have chosen to share numerous personal prayer experiences as they relate to the mobilizing of a specialized force of intercessors and foot soldiers committed to seeing the world evangelized in our generation. The purpose of these insights is to encourage and inspire the reader to become much more intimately involved in this harvest. Our generation could well witness what missiologists describe as "closure"* concerning Christ's command to evangelize the whole world.

And there is reason for optimism. The world is changing so rapidly that, in a period of less than eighteen months at the start of the final decade of the twentieth century, twenty-three new nations were formed, most resulting from the collapse of communism in Eastern Europe. With these changes have come remarkable open doors for the evangelization of those once restricted regions.

Could similar miracles be waiting on the horizon for other dark

---

* *Closure* is a term used to define the ultimate completion of the Great Commission whereby everyone on earth has had reasonable access to the gospel of Jesus Christ. Although no one could possibly know exactly when closure will be accomplished, many church leaders would link it to Christ's words in Matthew 24:14: "And this gospel of the kingdom will be preached in all the world as a witness to all nations, and then the end will come."

regions of the earth? In spiritual terms this is the Jericho hour. True, some of the remaining Jericho-type walls keeping the church from possessing its promise of reaching every tribe, tongue, people and nation with the gospel (Rev. 5:9-10) have yet to fall. But the mortar of centuries-long bondage clearly appears to be cracking, and the faint sounds of a shaking are coming from the distance. Let's take a closer look. *This is the Jericho hour.* ⌛

THE JERICHO HOUR

*Capturing the Momentum of
a Season of Suddenlies*

I WAS ill-prepared for the biting cold of that freezing Berlin evening. Moving toward the towering Berlin Wall, I wondered if anyone would recognize that I was dressed like a Californian from America who had little comprehension of what a real German winter was like.

I had traveled the almost six thousand miles from Los Angeles because of a five-word prayer assignment the Lord had given me in a late-night season of intercession. It had all begun forty-five days earlier, well past midnight, and was the conclusion of a month-long burden for the communist-controlled nations of Eastern Europe, a burden which had commanded the focus of my prayers almost daily.

Later my burden would birth a physical act of prayer that would take me to a higher level of strategic intercessory involvement and require the six-thousand-mile journey. But it started with a midnight prayer encounter. Tears were flowing as the words flooded my heart: "I want you to confront the strongholds of communism in Eastern Europe." I had heard this quiet voice before, and I knew God was speaking. But I didn't understand what it all meant.

"How, Lord?" was my simple question.

Clear instructions followed: "I want you to go to the Berlin Wall, lay your hands upon it and command it to come down in My name!"

My mind was flooded with the phrase "In Jesus' name, come down!" But I knew I had to travel in person to the wall to obey God's directive. True, prayer can go where God can go because prayer touches God, and God is everywhere; yet, for reasons beyond our understanding, God sometimes calls His children to on-site pilgrimages of prayer.

A chill swept over me as I approached the graffiti-covered western side of the Berlin Wall. I was glad my assignment was only five words and not a directive to spend a whole night in prayer at the wall! I felt little courage as I stepped toward this infamous monument to oppression. Indeed, as I reached to touch the wall I withdrew my hands quickly, my eyes darting to the right and left to see if anyone might be watching.

Shocked by my sudden sense of embarrassment, I realized I had come a considerable distance with a very simple, clear assignment. At once I pressed both hands to the huge wall and delivered my five-word prayer directive: "In Jesus' name, come down!" It was over in an instant.

In retrospect I wondered how a real man of faith — a George Müller, a Hudson Taylor or maybe a Charles Finney — might have prayed. I pictured one of these faith giants commanding the wall to fall and then rushing back from the towering structure to observe its imminent crumbling. But I just stood there. The fact is, I really didn't expect the wall to fall. Had it fallen, it would have crushed me. But, more significantly, the East German troops would have rushed to the break and simply reestablished this huge obstacle that stood as a mockery to freedom.

To be sure, I wasn't really speaking to a cement barrier, but rather to invisible forces of principalities and powers (see Eph. 6:12) that caused this structure to rise as a symbolic picture of communism's curtain of oppression.

That night, as I boarded a plane for the West, I wondered if my almost six-thousand-mile trip had been worth it. That was over a thousand miles for each word of my five-word prayer. As the plane ascended over the city of Berlin, my eyes caught two contrasting pictures below.

First, I saw a brightly lighted portion of the city that sparkled like a sea of glimmering diamonds. Then came sudden darkness — a region of blackness separated from the lighted area by a strange string of distant lights, stretching eerily across the heart of the city.

Immediately I realized what I was seeing. One side represented a free and brightly lighted Berlin. The dark side was East Berlin, where electricity was scarce and darkness came early. The visible had become a picture of the invisible. I felt I was witnessing the psalmist's words, "The dark places of the earth are full of the habitations of cruelty" (Ps. 74:20, KJV).

As the plane inched its way skyward, I wondered what, if anything, my prayer assignment had accomplished. Two weeks later, back home in freedom and comfort, I saw my first glimmer of hope. I gazed intently at the editorial in our local newspaper. Its headline read: "The Wall Behind the Wall Is Falling." The writer explained that, although the Berlin Wall still stood as a formidable symbol mocking human rights and freedom, the political dynamics that had kept that wall standing for so many years from behind the scenes was beginning to crumble from within. And although this editorial was speaking about political transitions, I knew that the prayers of the saints were making their impact.

Indeed, only sixty days would pass before Hungarian soldiers would be pictured on the front page of our papers cutting the barbed wire of their previously restricted borders. The wall behind the wall was indeed crumbling. The unraveling had begun. In another twenty-four months, the Soviet Union would cease to exist as a government. But my prayer assignment had just begun.

Youthful Warriors

After I arrived home from Berlin, I began praying daily regarding my next step in confronting the strongholds of communism in Eastern Europe. Instinctively I knew the Berlin trip was but a beginning. I soon received further instructions. My wife, Dee, and I were to take a team of intercessors to Eastern Europe that following summer to complete the assignment that had begun at the wall.

"Where will we find qualified intercessors for the journey?" I asked prayerfully.

The next impression first startled me and then filled my heart with special joy. "I want your team of intercessors to be teenagers," the Lord answered.

My joy was caused by the fact that our ministry to the nations had begun in our younger years as a prayer ministry mobilizing youth to pray. Almost two decades earlier we had begun a prayer center in Sacramento, California, for resident college-age youth who were asked to give a year of their lives to intercessory prayer. During a five-year period, God had sent a hundred young people to help staff the center.

Now, years later, the Lord was restoring in me a conviction that He desired to use young people mightily in His army of intercessors to change the world. A few days later I shared this burden with my pastor. He agreed that our church should help sponsor a specially trained group of young people who would go to Eastern Europe that following summer for warfare prayer. By summer, a total of twenty team members (average age, sixteen years) made the journey, joining my wife and me as we traveled to Eastern Europe. Two troubled communist nations were to be our focus — Romania and Bulgaria.

In Romania we chartered a bus and traveled along its main highway from one end of the country to the other, frequently reaching out our hands and praying for the villages as we passed by them. On occasion we would stop the bus for seasons of prayer in parks and secluded areas, something always done with cautious discretion; accompanying us was an official tour guide of Romania's communist government.

Upon our arrival at Bucharest, Romania's capital, we asked our guide for a free day to visit the city center. Secretly we planned to spend concerted time in warfare prayer throughout the Romanian capital. Our guide responded affirmatively, and the team was on its own, a miracle for that region of the world at that time. We took advantage of the victory and spent the day on various prayer walks throughout the city.

When we arrived at the huge, heavily guarded Communist party building in the center of the city, several team members had the same impression. We looked at the building and thought immediately of Jericho. We agreed this was a Jericho-like obstacle that required a Jericho-type prayer strategy. In moments, a prayer walk around the building had begun and continued six additional times until seven trips had been completed.

Did our prayers make a difference? Sixteen months later, members of our prayer team watched the evening news and saw that same building in flames. It was the last place from which Nicolae Ceausescu, Romania's ruthless leader, spoke to the Romanian people before being forced from power and, along with his wife, Elena, executed on Christmas Day, 1989, a few days later. Decades of oppression had ended in a few memorable moments. But history would show that God's people prayed. And, today, the very villages touched in prayer from a passing bus filled with youthful intercessors are being reached freely with the gospel, systematically, house-to-house. Did our prayers make a difference? The answer is obvious.

A Season of Suddenlies

As these remarkable transitions began unfolding, my wife attended a gathering of wives of Christian leaders in America. One felt the Lord had given her a personal "word" just prior to their meeting. It concerned Christ's body and the immediate future. "The church is about to move into a season of suddenlies," she declared, adding, "and I believe that obstacles Satan has raised up to keep people from the gospel will begin to crumble so quickly the church will hardly be able to handle the harvest."

We have, indeed, entered a season of suddenlies. According to George Otis Jr., author of the informative book *The Last of the Giants,* the progress of the Great Commission in our generation has been almost astounding.

Citing such recognized researchers as David Barrett, Otis explains that 70 percent of the progress made toward fulfillment of the Great Commission from the time Christ ascended into heaven until the 1990s has happened just since the beginning of the twentieth century. Further, 70 percent of that figure has happened since the end of World War II. And 70 percent of that latter figure has occurred in just the last thirty-six months.[1]

This clearly is the Jericho hour. Towering obstacles that have kept people from receiving the good news of Jesus Christ are falling so fast that it is almost impossible to pursue each new opportunity. Three decades ago the head of the Communist party, Nikita Khrushchev, declared that communism would bury us. Yet, by the last decade of the century, within just a few short months, the entire communist system disintegrated across Eastern Europe. It happened so quickly that even America's sophisticated intelligence community was confounded. America's secretary of state, James Baker III, would later testify that no one could have predicted so sudden a collapse. It was, he said, simply an act of God.

I believe it was one of God's suddenlies. So quick was the desire to remove every symbol of communism across the old Soviet Union that a shortage of cranes removing statues of Lenin had to be explained by government leaders to the complaining populace. A huge statue of Lenin in Kiev actually had an official government sign attached to it reading in Russian: "We are sorry for any temporary inconvenience."

God, indeed, delights in blessing His people with His sovereign suddenlies. *Suddenly* is an exciting word sprinkled throughout Scripture. Of resurrection morning the Bible tells us that as one of the disciples approached the empty tomb, "Suddenly Jesus met them" (Matt. 28:9, NIV). *Suddenly* speaks of immediacy while suggesting the miraculous. Jericho's falling walls were one of God's suddenlies. In the book of Chronicles, when Israel experienced one of its greatest spiritual awakenings, we are told Hezekiah and the people rejoiced that "God had prepared the people, since the events took place so suddenly" (2 Chr. 29:36).

In Jeremiah's judgment account of God's wrath on Babylon, it is said that Babylon had "suddenly" fallen (Jer. 51:8). Luke's account of Christ's birth says "suddenly" there was an angel with a multitude of heavenly host praising God (Luke 2:13). The day of Pentecost was another of God's suddenlies as a mighty rushing wind came "suddenly" from heaven (Acts 2:2). And the conversion of Saul of Tarsus who soon became Paul the apostle happened on the

Damascus road when "suddenly" a light shone on the future apostle (Acts 9:3).

Today's global "suddenlies" are changing the very scope of evangelistic activity almost daily as new hope abounds for the closure of Christ's commission in our generation.

A View From the Throne

I have often wondered what it would be like to be invited into the presence of the Lord, quite literally, to gaze across the earth's populace observing the totality of God's unfolding plan for global evangelization. In Revelation, John describes just such an invitation. After receiving the revelation of Christ's messages to the seven churches, John writes:

> After these things I looked, and behold, a door standing open in heaven. And the first voice which I heard was like a trumpet speaking with me, saying, "Come up here, and I will show you things which must take place after this" (Rev. 4:1).

If we, like the apostle John, could be ushered into God's presence to study, firsthand, the progress that is being made regarding the evangelization of the world, we would probably be astounded. As noted earlier, 70 percent of the meaningful plans developed for world evangelism since Christ gave His commission have been launched in the twentieth century. George Otis Jr. explains further that from 1961 to 1991 the tally of new global plans more than tripled the number launched over the first fifteen hundred years of church history.[2] According to Otis, 75 percent of the world's population now has a reasonable chance of hearing the gospel.[3]

Examples abound in the progress that the church is making in penetrating the dark places of the earth. In the ministry I direct, Every Home for Christ, in 1987 our seventy global offices received 206,923 written response cards from people impacted through the printed page. These cards represent people truly receiving Christ or requesting our four-part Bible correspondence course to pursue their desire to know Christ. Five years later that number had increased to 665,292 for the same twelve-month period. This encouraging increase of 221 percent happened in spite of the fact that our house-to-house literature distribution increased only a modest 34 percent over that same time frame. Other trends indicate that progress on closure is truly advancing.

According to Otis, twenty-one thousand parachurch or service agencies, along with more than two thousand Christian radio and TV stations, are now broadcasting the gospel regularly. In one recent year, over 50 million Bibles and New Testaments, along with 1.5 billion Scripture portions, were distributed. It is further estimated there are twenty-five hundred mass-evangelism campaigns such as those conducted by Billy Graham and Luis Palau every year in at least 1,300 cities and towns. Every Home for Christ annually visits every home with the gospel in an estimated 8,760 additional towns and villages each with an average population of ten thousand inhabitants.

Globally, Christ's body is advancing significantly. The church in Africa is said to be increasing by an average of twenty-five thousand believers daily. In China, alone, it is estimated that thirty-five thousand people are turning to Christ every day.

An equal number is finding Christ daily in Latin America. A Roman Catholic editor stated in the *Los Angeles Times* that if the present rate of conversions (by one estimate, four hundred per hour) to evangelical Christianity in Latin America continues unabated, by the end of the next century demographers predict that Latin America will be evangelical.[4]

In 1900, Africa was but 3 percent Christian. Today it is rapidly approaching 50 percent. Praise God — the church is halfway to its goal. (God is "not willing that *any* should perish," 2 Pet. 3:9, italics added.) In 1900, Korea had no Protestant churches. Today South Korea is 30 percent Christian, with more than seven thousand Christian churches in Seoul alone. Several of these have remarkable memberships, including one with 750,000 adherents and another with 250,000. Countries like Mongolia with few believers a decade ago are seeing such astounding growth that recent estimates indicated the church was doubling in size in Mongolia every ninety days.

As late as 1990, missiologists using a carefully established set of criteria to identify nations on earth with restricted access to the gospel listed Albania as the most-difficult-to-evangelize country in the world. By 1992 Every Home for Christ, with several other cooperating ministries, was participating in home-to-home evangelism to every home in Tirana, Albania's capital, with the official blessing of Albania's president. Scores of Albanians hand-delivered their decision cards to EHC's follow-up office in Tirana to be sure their responses would not be lost in the mail.

We have indeed entered a season of suddenlies. Jericho-type walls have been weakened and are falling. And clearly there is a relationship between the increased emphasis on strategic-level prayer (a term we'll explain later) and the spreading harvest.

Within months of a concerted, carefully planned, strategic prayer campaign focused on the city of La Plata in Argentina, pastor Samuel Desimone, director of Every Home for Christ's "Good News Behind Bars" campaign to reach every prisoner in Argentina, received an incredible report. It came from the warden of the notorious Olmos Prison. Over 30 percent of the inmates had genuinely converted to Christ. And so amazing was the change throughout the prison that only thirty of the regular three hundred contingent of prison guards were now needed to maintain order. The walls keeping people from the gospel are indeed falling everywhere.

True, prayer seems to have been chipping away at many of these walls for years, but "suddenly" God appears to be calling His children to much more pronounced levels of strategic warfare prayer that are hastening their crumbling. Perhaps my most unusual encounter of such prayer happened not at the Berlin Wall, but with our team of youthful intercessors on our prayer journey across Bulgaria.

Seeds of Glory

Following my journey to the Berlin Wall in January 1988 and the decision to take a team of praying young people to Eastern Europe that next summer, the team was carefully mobilized and trained for the pilgrimage. That following July we departed for the then communist-controlled countries of Romania and Bulgaria. I had asked one of our staff, Wes Wilson, to accompany us. He had previous experience in several short-term missions journeys with Youth With a Mission.

In addition to our Jericho-style prayer confrontation of Romania's Communist party headquarters described earlier, the team traveled by bus across Bulgaria. The oppression was so intense that all team members felt its weight. We had been told Bulgaria's communist leader, Todor Zhivkov, a strict Stalinist, had been in power longer than any dictator in Eastern Europe since Stalin.

Traveling across Bulgaria, our bus continued to be a prayer meeting on wheels as each village we passed was touched by intercession. We were heading from the Romanian border for the Bulgarian capital of Sofia. After arriving as tourists in a downtown hotel, we decided to visit the large central park of the capital and split up into several small groups for prayer. Soon the groups were scattered throughout the trees, interceding for the nation.

Wes Wilson, our other adult team leader, felt impressed to gather his group in a large clearing that was absent of people at that particular time of the day. God had given him a mental picture of a "physical" act he felt would release something of God's supernatural destiny over Bulgaria in the future.

Tearfully, Wes challenged each youth to dig a small hole in the ground as if to prepare for the planting of a seed. They responded readily, though one or two smiled as they thought of the strange act they were performing.

With the holes dug, Wes instructed each of the youthful warriors to reach toward heaven and grasp an invisible seed of God's glory and plant it in the ground. "Only a revelation of God's glory can save Bulgaria," he told them.

Tears soon filled the eyes of several of the group as they sensed the Holy Spirit was orchestrating this unusual activity. Each led in prayer, and the seeds were covered symbolically with a concluding time of praise.

Wes suddenly added a simple statement that months later would prove to be uniquely prophetic. "Someday I believe a revolution overthrowing communism will come to Bulgaria, and I believe it will begin right here on this very spot."

They were bold words that might have sounded as mere faith expressions of the moment. But what Wes said next was so measurable that all in the group perked up their ears. "I also believe that someday I'll read the answer to this prayer on the front page of the *Los Angeles Times*."

That following year, in mid-November, I arrived home from our California office late one night, collecting the *Times* just outside our door. With the paper in hand, I slumped into my easy chair both to catch my breath after a busy day and to catch up on the news. The Berlin Wall had "fallen" just four days earlier, and every day seemed to produce new and startling global developments. It was November 13, 1989. My eyes froze as I gazed at the front page of the *Los Angeles Times*. "Bulgarians Greet Change With Caution, Suspicion," the headline read.

My heart was beating hard as I began reading the article. It spoke of how "revolution" had come to Bulgaria and how it had all begun in a clearing in Sofia's large central park. These demonstrators had set up a table inviting Bulgarians to sign a petition opposing actions of their communist government in plans to divert the river flowing through their capital. The demonstrations and petition-signing were a ploy, the article explained, to allow people to vent their frustrations.

The initial group of signers was no more than the size of our team of intercessors. But that number would soon grow into hundreds and then thousands. The Bulgarian Revolution had begun! And, as the article explained, it all started in a clearing in Sofia's central park. I think some of our youthful intercessors might recognize that clearing!

The Jericho Hour

When the decade of the nineties began, the Berlin Wall had just crumbled, and the ruthless Romanian dictator, Nicolae Ceausescu and his wife, Elena, had just been executed. Communism was experiencing its demise in Eastern Europe. Still, few could have imagined that in less than twenty-four months, the Soviet Union as a government would no longer exist. During the height of the 1988 Summer Olympics in Seoul, Korea, had any student of global politics predicted that no Soviet flag would be flying in the next Olympics, such a person would have been labelled as crazy. Yet, at the 1992 Barcelona games, neither the Soviet flag flew nor did its once-proud national anthem ring out in recognition of gold-medal winners from the old Soviet Union.

"The Soviet Union Is Dead," read the headline on our local

newspaper just six weeks before the 1992 Winter Olympics began. Few mission strategists could possibly have imagined the dramatic changes that would likewise occur in such countries as Albania, Mongolia, Nepal, Nicaragua and Ethiopia. The wonder years of world evangelization are indeed upon us. Breakthroughs abound, and the harvest is hastening.

These dramatic falling walls remind us of God's intervention at Jericho in response to His people's obeying a simple, divinely ordained strategy. It was a miracle making possible the possessing of a promise. Today the great promise before the church is the evangelization of the world. That this objective will someday be realized is not in question. Isaiah prophesied, "The earth shall be full of the knowledge of the Lord as the waters cover the sea" (Is. 11:9). But for this to occur in our lifetime, every remaining barrier to the gospel must fall.

Recent miracles in once dark places globally give us cause for great hope. I truly believe this is the Jericho hour for the body of Christ. But we must capture the momentum of this season of suddenlies if our generation is to witness closure of the Great Commission. And the key to that closure is what we'll examine next. ⧗

TWO

PRAYING BACK
THE KING

*The Great Condition
to the Great Commission*

I WAS amazed that such a book could command so much attention. In but a few months' time, more than a million copies had been distributed. The title read simply *Eighty-eight Reasons Christ Will Return in 1988.*

Immediately the thought flooded my mind, Here we go again! If there's anything believers should have learned by now it is how absurd date-setting is when it comes to matters of Christ's return.

A year later, after Christ obviously had not returned in 1988, a Christian author and friend, Bob Hoskins, published a book with a most interesting title: *UNFINISHED: 2.7 Billion Reasons Jesus Didn't Come in 1988.*

I chuckled at the title even as I recognized at once the truth it conveyed. Jesus did, indeed, tell His disciples *when* He would return, but not in a time frame measured by man's calendar. Jesus made it clear His return was linked inseparably to the evangelization of the lost.

Mark describes the dialogue between Christ and His disciples regarding Christ's ultimate return to earth. The disciples queried:

> Tell us, when will *these things* be? And what will be *the sign* when all *these things* will be fulfilled? (Mark 13:4, italics added).

Interestingly, when the disciples used the plural word for "things" that would precede the end times and then referenced a specific "sign" (note the singular) regarding Christ's return, I believe the very tense of each expression was inspired by the Holy Spirit.

"When will these *things* be?" they asked.

Jesus answers them by sharing a variety of "things" (note again the plural) that will take place. He says many would come in His name saying they are Christ. He adds that wars and rumors of wars will occur as a part of the "things" that will happen. He then makes it clear that although all these things "must needs be...the end shall not be yet" (Mark 13:7, KJV).

Here it appears our Lord was suggesting these occurrences would happen over a relatively prolonged period. He continued by explaining that "nation shall rise against nation, and kingdom against kingdom." "Earthquakes, famine, and troubles" would likewise occur, but again our Lord suggests none of these "things" in and by themselves or taken collectively represent the telling "sign" of His imminent return. In fact, He simply explains, "These are the beginnings of sorrows" (Mark 13:8, KJV).

Suddenly a single definitive declaration comes from Christ's lips that is clearly different from His other remarks. It is the only direct prophetic statement in the narrative that refers specifically to the time of Christ's return. Jesus says simply, "And the gospel must first be published among all nations" (Mark 13:10, KJV).

The message is clear. Jesus will not return until the good news of His love is first published among "all nations." Further, we know this word *nations* carries the idea of people groups, of which hundreds are yet to be evangelized. Thus, the return of Christ is clearly related to closure of His Great Commission. And although God has His own sovereign timetable regarding the return of His Son, these passages would suggest that world evangelization is at the heart of it. Jesus seems to be saying, "If you don't go, I won't come!"

Matthew's rendering of these words of Christ in Mark 13:10 adds a significant six-word addition. We read:

> And this gospel of the kingdom will be preached in all the world as a witness to all the nations, *and then the end will come* (Matt. 24:14, italics added).

Here is the key to Christ's coming. His return is inseparably linked to the completion of the Great Commission. That the task will ultimately happen, as suggested in the last chapter, is abundantly clear from Scripture. The "revelation" that John saw includes a vision of multitudes redeemed by Christ's blood who come out of "every tribe and tongue and people and nation" (Rev. 5:9).

Why was John so sweeping in his report? He could have simply said, "I saw the redeemed come from throughout the world!" Instead, the apostle uses multiple expressions to be sure the reader understands the scope of the harvest. It isn't just "kinds" or tribes of lost souls that will be represented but *every* tribe. And, for added emphasis, all peoples (ethnic groups) likewise will be represented. Further, every geographic boundary (nations) will be touched along with every language and dialect. Of course, for this to occur, the earth will need to be saturated with the gospel in multitudes of languages along with saturation church-planting taking place among every people group.

But is it realistic to believe that any one generation could possibly accomplish so vast and complex a challenge? Is there a particular secret that might make it all happen? Perhaps the answer is to be found hidden in John's vision of Revelation 5:8-9 which we've been discussing.

In it we discover a small detail that is somewhat easy to overlook. As John describes the scope of the end-time harvest, he reports seeing "golden bowls full of incense, which are the prayers of the saints" (Rev. 5:8). Could this possibly be the key to closure?

Here is but one of two distinct passages in the book of Revelation referring to prayer-filled bowls or vials that are linked with end-time harvest events (see also Rev. 8:1-4). Each appears directly related to the unfolding of God's plan regarding the completion of Christ's bride and the ultimate establishment of His kingdom on earth. If these vials indeed are a key (if not *the* key) to the establishing of Christ's kingdom, what does all this mean for ordinary believers like you and me who genuinely care about the lost? And what bearing might this have on the strategic planning of praying people, churches and ministries who have a passion to see the fulfillment of the Great Commission in our generation?

Bringing Back the King

Oswald J. Smith, the renowned missionary statesman and pastor of the dynamic People's Church of Toronto, Ontario, and once honorary president of Every Home for Christ, preached a powerful sermon on world evangelization titled "Bringing Back the King." Citing Scripture verses shared earlier in this chapter (Mark 13:10; Matt. 24:14), Smith emphasized the fact that Christ simply would not return until the world was evangelized — period. He challenged listeners to get involved in fulfilling the Great Commission if they wanted to see the prophetic scenario of Christ's return unfold much more quickly. He also suggested that if Jesus said the end would come when the whole world heard the gospel, then let the whole world hear the message and watch what happens.

Today, in looking at the challenges of closure and facing the formidable remaining "giants" that stand in the way of its fulfillment, I am becoming increasingly convinced that the emerging global call to prayer will be the key to gathering in history's final and greatest harvest. To bring back the King, we must pray back the King.

Ministries like Every Home for Christ, with such challenging goals as mobilizing all of Christ's body to take a message of His love to every person, home by home, in every geographic region of the world, increasingly find their hands tied. Doors remain closed to vast arenas of unreached humanity because of ideological, political and religious strongholds. Something of a supernatural nature must occur to demolish these remaining strongholds and make possible the communicating of the good news by all ministries committed to this task if these vast multitudes are to hear of Christ's love in our generation. A single premise sums up my convictions on this matter of closure and the role strategic-level prayer (a term to be defined later) will play in the overall harvest:

> *God's ultimate purpose for mankind, the completion of Christ's bride and the establishing of His eternal kingdom on earth will result only from the release of the prayers of God's saints.*

From the earliest days following our Lord's commissioning of His disciples to evangelize the world, the role of prayer has been central to the task. Christ Himself established prayer's centrality in His only specific recorded assessment of the harvest challenge to be found in the Gospels. "The harvest truly is plentiful, but the laborers are few," He said (Matt. 9:37). The problem was simple — too many people, too few workers. In an instant, Jesus provided the solution: "Therefore pray the Lord of harvest to send out laborers into His harvest" (Matt. 9:38).

The role of prayer in the harvest is later stressed by our Lord when He appears to His followers just prior to His ascension. Forty days had passed since His resurrection, and He is now about to leave His disciples. It is time to give them their final evangelistic assignments.

Luke describes this commissioning session in the opening words of his Acts of the Apostles. Many disciples had assembled for the occasion. Although the account in Acts does not specifically number those present, many Bible scholars believe this is the occasion referred to by Paul in 1 Corinthians 15:6, where Christ is described as appearing to five hundred disciples at one time following His resurrection.

If such is an accurate assumption, it is a rather revealing fact. Here Christ is commissioning His disciples to go into all the world and communicate the gospel to every creature. However, before they can "go," they must "wait"! Note first the directive:

> And being assembled together with them, He [Jesus] commanded them not to depart from Jerusalem, but to wait for the Promise of the Father, "which," He said, "you have heard from Me" (Acts 1:4).

26

Obedience to this directive, our Lord explains, will give release to a promise of power:

> But you shall receive power when the Holy Spirit has come upon you; and you shall be witnesses to Me in Jerusalem, and in all Judea and Samaria, and to the end of the earth (Acts 1:8).

Significant to the narrative is the actual number responding to Christ's commission. About 120 disciples eventually participated in the ten-day upper room encounter (Acts 1:15). If five hundred followers of Christ had indeed heard the challenge, only 24 percent responded. Apparently the remaining 76 percent (a three-quarters majority) had other things to do. They had missed the significance of the prayer factor in obeying Christ's commission. And if it was essential at the outset, it will most certainly be essential for closure.

Angels and Vials

Regarding closure and the role prayer plays in it, we need to look again at the apostle John's prophetic picture of the angels and the vials (see Rev. 5:8-9; 8:1-4). Something interesting unfolds concerning the relationship of those prayer-filled bowls and the release of angels into the heavenlies to carry out God's directives. It appears that the rise of prayer relates to the release of angels.

Consider the last great heavenly battle between Satan's demonic powers and the Lord's angelic army (see Rev. 12:7-11). Although prayer is not specifically mentioned in these verses, the point of release for all of these unfolding events is clearly the bringing of the vials or bowls of prayer before the altar of God as recorded in Revelation 8:1-4. Here we discover the commissioning of seven angels who give release to key elements pertaining to what might be termed the wrap-up of this present age.

First, it must be understood that the supernatural warfare of Revelation 12:7-11 is directly related to the trumpet announcement of the seventh angel whose blast accompanies a proclamation:

The kingdoms of this world have become the kingdoms

of our Lord and of His Christ, and He shall reign forever
and ever! (Rev. 11:15).

It is this seventh angel, sounding a trumpet, that heralds the
release of this reality.

Further, there is a clear linkage between the loud voices of Revelation 11:15 and the warfare victory of Revelation 12:10 where we read:

> Then I heard a loud voice saying in heaven, "Now salva-
> tion, and strength, and the kingdom of our God, and the
> power of His Christ have come, for the accuser of our
> brethren, who accused them before our God day and
> night, has been cast down."

Indeed, the "loud voice" of Revelation 12:10 could well be the
same "loud voices" as recorded in Revelation 11:15. The latter may
be but a more detailed explanation of the former.

This casting down of Satan in Revelation 12:10 then becomes the
result of a great spiritual battle between the armies of heaven, led
by Michael the archangel, and the armies of hell, led by Satan
himself. In the battle, heaven's angelic warriors expel Satan and his
demonic troops forever from the invisible, heavenly realm. They
are, as Scripture says, "cast down."

It is important to note, however, that this victory against the
"accuser of our brethren" (Rev. 12:10) was not achieved solely by
the angels, but rather by the application of spiritual weaponry
administered by believers on earth. True, the angels did the fighting, but God's saints provided the fire power. This is clear by the
words of verse 11:

> And they overcame him [Satan] by the blood of the Lamb
> and by the word of their testimony....

The angels per se did not overcome the accuser; rather, the
saints did, even though the angels were God's means for adminis-
tering the victory.

Of particular significance is the relationship of the prayers released in Revelation 8:3 (typified by the vials), along with much
worship offered (typified by the incense) to the unfolding of this

angelic activity specifically regarding the sounding of the seven trumpets. These trumpeting angels set in motion events that lead to the decisive spiritual victory of Revelation 12:10-11.

Only when the seventh angel sounds with the trumpet, accompanied by the loud voices, does Christ's kingdom finally come. From that moment, according to Scripture, Christ shall reign forever and ever (Rev. 11:15). But what gave release to this angel, and the other six, to sound their trumpets? Surely if it can be shown that prayer was instrumental in the commissioning of the angels to sound their trumpets, it might also be concluded that prayer plays a significant role in the saints' applying the "blood of the Lamb and the word of their testimony" leading to the ultimate victory of Revelation 12:11.

To describe prayer's role in the unfolding of these events, we must trace our steps back to the initial commissioning of the seven angels with their trumpets as recorded in Revelation 8:1-2. John writes:

> When He [the Lamb] opened the seventh seal, there was silence in heaven for about half an hour. And I saw the seven angels who stand before God, and to them were given seven trumpets.

Here the angels are given the trumpets but are not yet permitted to use them. Something must happen first which appears related to their release. The testimony continues:

> Then another angel, having a golden censer, came and stood at the altar. He was given much incense, that he should offer it with the prayers of all the saints upon the golden altar which was before the throne (Rev. 8:3).

A Season of Silence

Regarding the unexplained season of silence recorded in Revelation 8:1 that precedes the breaking of the prayer vials, writer Walter Wink explains:

> Heaven itself falls silent. The heavenly hosts and celestial spheres suspend their ceaseless singing so that the

prayers of the saints on earth can be heard. The seven angels of destiny cannot blow the signal of the next times to be until an eighth angel gathers these prayers...and mingles them with incense upon the altar. Silently they rise to the nostrils of God.

Human beings have intervened in the heavenly liturgy. The uninterrupted flow of consequences is dammed for a moment. New alternatives become feasible. The unexpected becomes suddenly possible, because God's people on earth have invoked heaven, the home of the possibles, and have been heard. What happens next, happens because people prayed. The message is clear: history belongs to the intercessors.[1]

It is indeed only after the smoke of the incense (Rev. 8:4), a biblical symbol of worship, is combined with the prayers of all the saints (Rev. 8:4), that the angel takes the censer, fills it with fire and casts it upon the earth. Thus, as the result of the prayers of God's people, saturated with much worship, the seven angels are permitted to sound their trumpets. They progress in their assignments until the final trumpet heralds the fullness of Christ's coming kingdom along with the accompanying cleansing of the heavenlies of demonic forces as described in Revelation 12:7-11.

Of fundamental significance is the fact that these seven angels give progressive release to the culmination of Christ's kingdom and that prayer released from heavenly vials begins this release. Indeed, Revelation 10:7 says of this seventh trumpeting angel:

But in the days of the sounding of the seventh angel, when he is about to sound, the mystery of God would be finished, as He declared to His servants the prophets.

Could it be that the "mystery of God" referred to here is the final culmination of the completion of Christ's bride, which most certainly is the ultimate goal God has in mind for His Son? If so, we suddenly discover the awesome significance of the release of prayer as it relates to the ultimate evangelization of the world and the full revelation of Christ's eternal kingdom on earth.

Also of significance in this warfare lesson of Revelation 12:7-11 is the mention of Michael the archangel. This is but one of four occasions in which Michael is mentioned in Scripture. Other passages include Daniel 10:13,21; Daniel 12:1; and Jude 9. In each of these passages, as with the Revelation 12 account, spiritual warfare is clearly implied. Especially noteworthy is the Daniel passage where Michael's involvement in a decisive spiritual victory is the direct result of Daniel's unwillingness to give up in prayer until the full answer comes (see Dan. 10:12-13).

It appears that prayer at levels perhaps never understood or applied in past generations will be key to closure and the completion of the task of global evangelization. It is, quite simply, the great condition to the Great Commission. As Graham Kendrick and Chris Robinson wisely wrote in their hymn *All Heaven Waits:*

> All heaven waits with bated breath for saints on earth
>   to pray,
> Majestic angels ready stand with swords of fiery blade.
> Astounding power awaits a word from God's resplen-
>   dent throne.
> But God awaits our prayer of faith that cries, "Your will
>   be done."[2] ⧖

THREE

DIVINE COINCIDENCES

*A Fresh Perspective
on the Nature of Prayer*

RICHARD TRENCH, archbishop of Dublin, once was reportedly confronted by a skeptic who questioned the prelate's testimonies of answered prayer.

"Your answers to prayer are nothing but coincidences," scoffed the skeptic.

"Whether my answers to prayer are coincidences or not, I know not," Trench promptly replied. "I only know this: The more I pray, the more coincidences I have, and the less I pray, the less coincidences I have." With a smile he concluded, "So I'll just keep on praying and watch all these coincidences keep on happening."

Prayer, on the surface, is as simple as talking to a friend. Yet, when we study this discipline in depth, we discover a multitude of complexities as our answers to prayer unfold. It seems the moment we grasp what appears to be a reasonable understanding of the theology of prayer, God sends an answer that forces us to rethink our positions.

Look carefully at some of our answers to prayer. Often, long before we ever thought to pray a particular petition, God set in motion certain events so that our prayer, when finally prayed, would be answered. Further, when examining some of these answers to our prayers, it becomes obvious that, even though God set in motion the answer before we actually prayed for a need, had we not prayed, certain circumstances could well have prevented our ever seeing the answer. Sound confusing? Consider this.

John Aycock, a gifted trial attorney in Tennessee, had just retired from his successful lifelong practice. Upon retirement, he contacted our Every Home for Christ office regarding some type of volunteer position where he might serve the ministry meaningfully. Because he had a special heart for prayer, we suggested he become involved as a coordinator of our ministry's Change the World School of Prayer, a multi-hour prayer training course.[1]

John agreed to become one of our first video coordinators with the assignment of presenting the Change the World School of Prayer by video in smaller churches where "live" instructors might not be able to go because of the expense. To these smaller settings, we could afford to send volunteer coordinators along with the video tapes of the sessions because each was responsible for his or her own personal support.

In one of John's first assignments, he was to coordinate the seminar at a respected Southern Baptist church in a modest Arkansas community. He arrived at the church about eight o'clock on a Monday morning to prepare for the three-night school of prayer scheduled to begin that evening. He had been told in advance that about seventy-five people would attend.

John was excited when he met the young pastor who explained that nearly their entire adult congregation had registered for the seminar and paid the tuition. Now, instead of the expected seventy-five people attending, hundreds would attend. To the pastor it was a miracle. But to John it was a potential catastrophe.

He had actually come early that morning to prepare all the

manuals, workbooks and other materials, along with the overhead projector and large-screen television for the training that evening. Now his heart was filled with considerable anxiety.

His feeling of panic was triggered by the many hours of training he had experienced in order to serve as a coordinator. He had attended at least five seminars for this training where he watched in detail the ingredients that helped make the seminar successful. He learned that no school of prayer could be presented successfully without using all the materials precisely as intended. Obviously with a severe shortage of manuals for that night's seminar the entire event seemed doomed to failure.

John shared his concern with the pastor, explaining that it was impossible to present the school of prayer effectively without the materials.

"Why don't you call your office and have the materials flown in?" the pastor asked.

John told him that even if the materials were put on a plane immediately, they wouldn't arrive until the following day. He again reminded the pastor that these materials were absolutely essential to the effectiveness of the study.

Little did John realize that God was preparing him for one of the most unusual answers to prayer he would ever experience.

"Well, Brother John," the pastor asked, "if you can't get the materials here on time, what are you going to do?"

John's confident reply came without hesitation, "I'm going to ask God for a miracle!"

Moments later John was on his face in the darkened sanctuary of the Baptist church. "How can I present a school of prayer that teaches people You answer prayer if this prayer goes unanswered?" he pleaded with God. "And You've got to answer quickly, God, because You have only until 7:00 P.M. tonight."

John suddenly leaped to his feet. He didn't understand why he felt such an urgency to end his prayer. He glanced at his watch. It was exactly 12:00 noon.

He got into his car and, as if directed by an invisible force, headed across town. Driving down the town's main street, which ran just adjacent to the interstate freeway, he was overwhelmed with the simple recognition that God had His perfect solution for this very specific problem. He didn't know how, but he knew God would respond. Almost instinctively, he cried out, "God, whatever shall I do?"

To his amazement God not only answered him, but He chose to do so in an audible voice. Interestingly, John came from a spiritual background where hearing God speak was considered highly suspect. Only deranged people heard "voices." He couldn't remember a single Christian friend who ever spoke of hearing God's voice audibly. Some might accept His speaking to the hearts of His children in quiet whispers, but speaking audibly was reserved for an earlier generation.

Later, John shared his experience with me, explaining somewhat reluctantly about hearing so clear a voice. I sensed he may have wondered what I felt about such a manifestation. I urged him on, and he told the whole story.

"He spoke just three words, Brother Dick — only three words."

"What did He tell you, John?" I asked.

Hesitating a moment, he continued, "It's just so hard to believe." After considerable prodding, he finally said, "Well, Brother Dick, God said simply, 'Turn into McDonald's.' "

Now I understood why he was so reluctant to share his experience. Here was a truly credible brother I knew well who actually heard God speak, and all He had said to him were three words, "Turn into McDonald's!"

"Was there a McDonald's?" I asked. After all, the town wasn't that large, and perhaps it was one of the few places in America where the restaurant chain had yet to make its mark. Of course, if there were no McDonald's, surely God hadn't spoken.

John laughed and said yes, adding that McDonald's was one of the few distinctive landmarks along the main street.

"What did you do?"

"I drove into McDonald's as fast as I could and practically ran into the restaurant," John added.

"What happened next?"

"I ordered fries and a coffee."

"Did God say anything else?"

"No, not another word!"

"You mean that's the end of the whole story?" I asked.

"Oh, no. That's when I heard another voice!"

"I thought God didn't say anything else."

"Oh, it wasn't God's voice I heard next," John said, "but it was just as shocking!"

He certainly had my undivided attention.

"It came from directly behind me, and I recognized it immediately."

"What did this voice say?" I asked almost cynically.

"The voice said, 'Daddy, Daddy, Daddy!' " Standing behind him were his nineteen-year-old daughter, Elizabeth, and her college classmate, Mary Lee Ferguson, hundreds of miles from both the college they were attending and home. For a moment John felt as if he were dreaming.

"What on earth are you doing here?" he asked his daughter.

She responded with her own question: "What are you doing here?"

"I asked you first," John said, and they both started to laugh.

"Daddy, don't you remember this is our week of spring break? We finished our exams earlier than expected, and Mary Lee wanted to get home early to see her fiancé and plan for her wedding."

Before John could catch his breath, his daughter asked a question that in retrospect appeared clearly to be prompted by the Holy Spirit: "Well, Daddy, how's everything going?"

Until that moment John had actually forgotten his difficult dilemma. He had even forgotten how he had ended up at the counter of that specific McDonald's restaurant. His face now showed concern as he responded, "Not very well, honey. Not very well at all."

"Daddy, what's wrong?" Elizabeth asked.

John explained how he was in that community to direct a Change the World School of Prayer for a local Baptist church and how almost the entire congregation had registered to attend. He then explained how he had just learned that without a miracle most of the participants would not have manuals for the evening because not enough had arrived.

"Honey, I just don't know what I'm going to do," he said.

Instantly, Elizabeth began to laugh — hardly the response he had anticipated. "Daddy, this may be just an amazing coincidence, but I think Mary Lee's trunk is full of everything you need."

John didn't understand. How could she possibly have what he needed? Before he could ask, Elizabeth continued.

"Daddy, what you probably don't know is that several weeks ago my pastor asked me if I would help coordinate a Change the World School of Prayer in the Tulsa area, and I agreed. But somehow they ordered far more manuals than needed — hundreds, in fact."

Elizabeth was excited as she gave the details of how the manuals ended up in Mary Lee's trunk. "When the school of prayer instructor, Ray Beeson, learned that I was your daughter, he suggested that I take the manuals home to you, and perhaps you could store them in your garage. Ray felt this would save shipping costs for the ministry in the long run.

"Daddy," she concluded, "Mary Lee agreed to let me fill her trunk with those manuals. We didn't even bring home any suitcases. I think the trunk is filled with all the materials you need for tonight's seminar."

John couldn't believe what he was hearing as the three of them rushed to the parking lot. He stood almost breathless as the trunk was opened. Counting the items confirmed the significance of the miracle. There were just enough manuals and workbooks for those who had registered for the seminar.

Tears were impossible to contain as John told his daughter, "Honey, this is one of the greatest miracles I have ever seen in my life." He then explained how he had cried out to God only a short distance up the street and how God had spoken just three words audibly: "Turn into McDonald's."

"How amazing," he said, "that you drove by at that same exact second."

"It's more amazing than you think, Daddy," Elizabeth said. "You see, last night I had loaned all my cash to a friend who needed help to go home for spring break. I had fully intended to go to the bank early this morning and cash a check to help Mary Lee with gas money. But then I overslept terribly this morning — by three hours, in fact. Mary Lee was furious. She was in a hurry to get home to her fiancé, so I decided to forget about the bank.

"It wasn't until we were well underway and very hungry that we realized all we had were a couple of dollars in change, no credit card and no cash. We both started to cry and pray at the same time. We knew we couldn't go another ten or fifteen miles. And that's when we saw a sign — 'McDonald's, 8 miles ahead.' We decided that at least we had enough coins to buy some french fries."

Elizabeth concluded with excitement, "Daddy, if I hadn't overslept, and if we hadn't been so hungry and nearly out of gas, and if it hadn't been for that sign, we couldn't possibly have shown up here at this moment."

As John finished telling me his amazing testimony, he asked, "Dick, have you ever heard of a miracle like this in all of your life?"

In that instant the Holy Spirit flooded my heart with a fresh revelation of the nature of prayer.

"John," I asked, "do you realize just how miraculous your miracle was?"

He had a quizzical look on his face as I explained. "First, your daughter had to attend a particular university that would make it necessary while traveling home to pass by that specific community. Then she had to be traveling with a classmate also from your hometown who would happen to fall in love with a young man — resulting in wedding plans that would require her to get home as quickly as possible. Then your daughter would need to give away all her cash the night before the trip, as well as oversleep the next morning so she couldn't go to the bank to cash a check. This would require a stop at the very town where you would be teaching a Change the World School of Prayer at that Baptist church."

John listened intently while I continued, "Don't forget that Elizabeth had to agree to coordinate a school of prayer in her city that was easily scheduled more than six months before you ever prayed your prayer. And the planners of that event had to order far too many manuals and workbooks for their event, which, coincidentally, would be the exact number you would need many months later in a similar event that was not yet even scheduled."

John's eyes widened as I added, "And we can't overlook the fact that the school of prayer instructor who taught that seminar would suggest that Elizabeth take the extra manuals to you rather than send them to the Every Home for Christ office."

"And, John, to top it all off, as many as ten to fifteen years before you would ever think to cry out to God while driving down that city street, workmen had to erect a sign outside that specific community that read 'McDonald's — 8 miles ahead' just to answer your prayer."

A Future of Hope

God clearly delights in answering the prayers of His children. When He spoke through Jeremiah to His people regarding their eventual deliverance from their Babylonian captivity, He declared:

> For I know the plans I have for you...plans to prosper you and not to harm you, plans to give you hope and a future (Jer. 29:11, NIV).

Although it may seem that answered prayers are often instantaneous, a more careful look reveals that God is constantly involved in the process of bringing about these answers.

Look again at my friend John. Had he not called out to God seeking guidance at the precise moment he did, he would not have heard God's audible response, "Turn into McDonald's." And if he had not gone into McDonald's when he did, he might never have known that his daughter and her roommate had stopped at that same location with a trunk full of the very materials he needed for his seminar. Clearly, God had set up a remarkable answer to a prayer that might never have been answered had John not cried out desperately to God at the exact moment when he did.

I believe many such apparent coincidences are actually divine appointments for answered prayer — but that they happen only if we pray.

A miracle "flight" out of Bombay, India, represents one such personal encounter. It happened as I was traveling throughout Asia on behalf of Every Home for Christ. I had finished conducting a missions conference in Sri Lanka after which I was to fly immediately to Bombay, India. From there, after an overnight stay, I was to travel on to my final destination of Katmandu, Nepal. Inadequate airline connections necessitated my overnight stay in Bombay at a hotel adjacent to the airport.

That next afternoon I was to catch an Air India flight to New Delhi that was supposed to connect me just in time with a Royal Nepal flight into Katmandu. With a little spiritual luck (if there is such a thing), I hoped to arrive just in time for a major national conference in a country where such meetings were banned only twenty-four months earlier.

A good night's sleep was a welcome blessing after arriving in Bombay. I rejoiced in realizing I could sleep as late as I wished because my plane didn't depart until mid-afternoon. By ten o'clock I was restfully engaged in a special season of prayer, having slept until almost nine.

I had planned to spend the entire morning in God's Word and prayer when suddenly I felt an overwhelming urge to depart immediately for the airport. It was a strange feeling. I had already contacted the hotel desk inquiring about what time I should depart for the airport since I had a mid-afternoon flight. I was told to leave after 1 P.M. Still I could not remove this urgent feeling from my mind. Instantly I gathered up all my luggage and rushed for the airport.

To my amazement the Air India terminal appeared completely deserted. I saw not a single passenger or airline agent. Every counter was vacant. I gazed at the giant electronic board announcing that day's departures. There was only one flight listed — the flight I was to take. But beside the flight number was a single word that brought an instant sense of panic — *delayed*. The new flight time was also listed — 23:30 (or 11:30 P.M. that night). I would miss my critical connection by more than eight hours.

It seemed that I was the only passenger who had not heard the flight had been delayed by half a day. And I had actually arrived several hours before the original departure time. It never occurred to me that God had planned all this just to answer my morning prayers for His guidance.

I walked to an empty airline counter and stood silently alone as if expecting something to happen. To my amazement and surprise it did. A door beside a mirrored window just behind the counter opened, and from it stepped an Air India agent. Apparently, she had observed me from behind the window.

"May I be of help?" she asked politely.

I explained my dilemma and asked if she might direct me to another flight that would enable me to make my connection on time. Because I had arrived so much earlier than the previously announced departure time of my now delayed flight, I held out hope of catching another plane.

She explained quietly that no other flights were scheduled to depart for New Delhi until much later that afternoon. None would arrive in time for me to connect with my 6 P.M. flight for Katmandu.

What happened next both surprised and troubled me. I began to insist that the agent find a plane that would take me that afternoon to New Delhi. It was generally not my nature to speak sharply, let alone demand the impossible. Still I said firmly, "You must find a plane that will take me to New Delhi, and you must find it for me now."

I can still recall the shocked look on the agent's face as she responded, "Would you wait for just a moment?" She retreated at once through the same door from which she had emerged earlier. Although feeling guilty for speaking so sternly, I waited as instructed. Less than five minutes had passed when she once again appeared, this time holding a single boarding pass. She handed it to me with a smile and motioned toward the customs and immigration area, explaining that I should proceed quickly in order to catch the plane.

I couldn't believe what I was hearing. I asked her what plane she was talking about, and she turned and pointed through huge glass windows at a giant 747 sitting idly by a gate. It was the only plane anywhere to be seen. She said it was a nonscheduled plane that a day earlier had been pulled from service because of mechanical problems. Now it was fully repaired and was to be flown to New Delhi. Later that evening it would become an international flight going to Frankfurt, Germany. But first it had to be taken to New Delhi. "We will take you on that plane," she said.

I was absolutely stunned as I walked alone through customs and immigration holding a boarding pass to a flight that didn't actually exist. Initially, not even a customs agent was in the area to check me through, and I had walked well past the immigration desk when an agent saw me and came running to catch me. When he saw my boarding pass, he proceeded to tell me the flight I was heading for had been cancelled and wouldn't be flying. I explained to him that an agent had just given me the pass and had instructed me to go and get on the plane. He wouldn't believe me and ushered me back to the airline agent.

Much to the officer's surprise, I had indeed been the only passenger cleared from the delayed flight to go through customs at that time. He again led me back through the immigration area to put me on a flight that technically didn't exist.

As I flew to New Delhi that afternoon, I rejoiced at the marvelous miracle that had begun earlier that morning. I now understood why I had felt so strongly impressed in prayer to leave at once for the airport.

But the best of the day's blessings was yet to come. In all of the intensity and anxiety of the moments prior to boarding the unscheduled flight, I had paid little attention to the time. I took out my itinerary and noticed that I had originally been scheduled to land at 5:05 P.M., which would have been just enough time to connect with my 6 P.M. departure for Katmandu. Not knowing exactly how long this unplanned flight would be, I wondered if I would reach New Delhi on time.

Suddenly the huge plane started its descent for landing. The plane was soon on the ground and began a journey of several minutes along the taxi way toward the terminal. I was getting anxious. As the huge plane lurched to a stop at the gate, I looked at my watch. The minute hand struck exactly five minutes past 5 P.M. I had arrived to the very second of my originally scheduled flight on a nonscheduled aircraft that should have been in New Delhi a day earlier. And it had all begun in prayer — just another of those divine coincidences! ☸

FOUR

WARFARE REALITIES

*Coming to Grips With
the Nature of Our Conflict*

OR MORE than three hours through an interpreter, the two Every Home for Christ field evangelists reasoned from Scripture with the five village elders. It was their first attempt to penetrate the previously unevangelized Kwaio people of a mountainous region of the Solomon Islands, a Pacific island chain consisting of a hundred inhabited islands. At times, the young men feared for their lives and with sufficient reason.

The first British government representative to venture into the region almost seventy years earlier was murdered within days of his arrival. That act prompted a British naval ship to bombard the region, killing many Kwaio, who became even more hostile to outsiders. In more recent years three Catholic priests suffered martyrdom while seeking to visit the area. The first was slain on the very day he arrived. The other two were brutally murdered within a few days of beginning their mission.

The Roman Catholic archbishop of the Solomons had shared these facts at an interchurch conference in Honiara, the capital city of the Solomon Islands, following an amazing breakthrough among these fiercely independent people. He chose the occasion of the conference to commend the brave young Protestant workers for their miraculous victories amongst the Kwaio. He also noted their willingness to risk their lives in taking the knowledge of Jesus to these previously unreached people.

And it all began with that initial encounter of several hours with the five village elders, called "lesser chiefs" in the language of the region. The two workers had been captured a short time earlier by several strong warriors of the village who apparently helped guard the "high chief," who lay gravely ill. The evangelists were immediately taken to the high chief's residence where the five elders were holding deliberations in a room adjacent to where the old chief was dying.

The chief was especially respected because, in addition to being the supreme authority of the area, he was also a priest (or witch doctor) who was said to have special powers that came from offering sacrifices to demons.

The two Christian workers were ushered into the large room where the five elders met. Recognizing the authority possessed by the old chief, the young evangelists repeatedly requested permission to meet with the revered leader. They had learned from campaigns in other islands that once a head chief grants permission to conduct any kind of business, no villagers could hinder their activities. But with each request to see the chief came a firm refusal. He was too ill, they were told.

Hours passed as the workers reasoned with the elders regarding the claims of Christ, all the while repeating their appeal to meet directly with the chief. When the workers pressed the elders to accept Christ as the only Son of God, they steadfastly refused, saying they would only accept what the high chief believed.

Suddenly, the first miracle occurred. The elders consented to allow the two young men to spend a brief time with the high chief.

As they entered the chief's room, they viewed a frail old man whom they estimated to be well over a hundred years old. He was lying in his traditional "earth bed" which had been carved out of the ground floor of his private bedroom.

Surprisingly, the old chief listened attentively to the message brought by the evangelists. It was as if he had waited a lifetime to hear this strange but glorious news of eternal life. Without questioning the message, the old chief did what the young men encouraged him to do. He repeated a simple sinner's prayer asking Jesus Christ, God's only Son, to come into his heart. Then, to the shock of the young workers, as well as the village elders, the old chief closed his eyes and died!

Commotion filled the chief's residence as the elders realized what had happened. Naturally, the workers were blamed for bringing some kind of a curse of their "religion" into the chief's room, resulting not in his healing but his death. Now, facing their own imminent deaths, the evangelists decided they might as well proclaim the gospel as zealously as possible. In the meantime, the lifeless body of the old chief lay only a few feet away.

More than two hours passed as all sense of time was forgotten in the strange atmosphere of a fervent dialogue that was clearly being orchestrated by the Holy Spirit. Suddenly, to the stunned amazement of all present, the old chief revived and sat straight up. It was as if he had experienced a sudden burst of divine resurrection energy.

Now the commotion was one of almost heart-stopping awe. The old chief promptly called for his entire family and friends to come and listen to what he had to say. In minutes, scores of villagers spilled out of his crowded residence.

The elderly patriarch then recounted his strange and overwhelming experience. He told his subjects that, upon dying, he had been met by, in his own words, "a man dressed brilliantly in white with wings." Apparently, the tribe had no specific word in their language for "angel." He further explained that this strange being took him to a place where great multitudes were worshipping the man called Jesus, the person to whom he had earlier surrendered his life in prayer.

The chief then explained how he was introduced to Abraham, Elijah and other prophets which he specifically mentioned by name — a remarkable thing considering there is no record of any portion of the Bible ever coming to these villages.

The old man continued his strange testimony, describing how he was shown a place where people were in great distress, crying, pleading and groaning. The chief had no word for "hell" in his vocabulary but vividly described a place not unlike a traditional biblical view of Hades. According to the chief, the heavenly messenger pointed toward this dreadful place, saying, "That's where those who reject Jesus go." He then pointed back toward the joyous throng worshipping Christ and declared, "Those who accept Jesus go there!"

The being in white then told the chief it was necessary for him to return for a time to his people. He must tell them to stop worshipping their false gods and to hear and believe the message the two young men had brought to their village.

"By receiving this message about Jesus," the angel told the chief, "the people of your village will reach this place." The angel pointed in the direction of the worshipping multitude.

As the old chief finished relating his incredible adventure, he turned to the two young Christian workers and told them to tell everyone the same message about Jesus they had shared with him earlier. Then, just as suddenly as it had all begun, the old chief died again. This time he was not to be revived. He had been alive just two hours, but that was all the time that was needed for the Holy Spirit to complete His work. In those moments, every person present prayed to receive Christ as Savior, including the five lesser chiefs who earlier had rejected the message.

Word of the miracle spread through the whole region, and hundreds of villagers turned to Christ. Within several weeks, nine fellowships of new believers had begun in an area where, before May 14, 1990, there had never been a reported gospel witness. In the old chief's village, three hundred converts now gather weekly for worship and Bible teaching. Today, there are thirty-six additional smaller fellowships of believers and fourteen fully functioning churches. From that first convert of the priestly chief have come over four thousand converted tribesmen. It's a miracle that reads as if it came directly from the pages of the book of Acts.

But this harvest throughout a once ferocious mountain tribe didn't happen just by accident. Days before those miraculous events occurred in the high chief's residence, Every Home for Christ workers from both Fiji and the Solomon Islands had been visiting villages in the coastlands of this large island. Here numerous distant relatives of the mountain Kwaio had come to Christ, but they, too, greatly feared their fellow tribesmen living in the dense jungle mountains that had never been penetrated with the gospel.

When the coastal work concluded, one of the Christian workers from Fiji asked when the work might be carried into the mountains. He was told that no one dared go into the mountain region because death would most certainly befall them. Intense discussions resulted as to what it meant to obey Christ's commission fully. Did it not include going into all the world, even if it meant risking one's life?

The entire group agreed that when Jesus told His disciples to give "every creature" the good news, His commission included the Kwaio peoples in the mountains. But they also realized they would have a spiritual battle on their hands because the region had most certainly been controlled by demonic forces for centuries. It was agreed that seven days would be set aside for prayer and fasting.

As the seven days unfolded, supernatural insights flowed into the hearts of the praying workers. Discernment and knowledge came regarding a host of demonic spirits and principalities controlling the region. Strange-sounding names were revealed in prayer, and as each was identified the workers would pray fervently until a sense of victory came.

One of the leaders kept count of these confrontations, and before the seven days had passed eighty-seven "strongholds" had been identified and dealt with in prayer. Only then did the workers feel spiritually prepared to move into those treacherous mountains. They seemed to understand that dealing with the darkness through fasting and prayer was the most essential step in establishing a point of entry for the light of the gospel into the region.

Understanding the Darkness

Of course, in order to penetrate the darkness with any meaningful prayer strategy, we must first understand the nature of the battle. Because we live in a physical world, it is often easy to address issues concerning human suffering, especially regionally and nationally, in terms that are primarily physical.

The devastating famine that swept across regions of North Africa in the early and mid-1980s is a prime example. At a time when famine seemed to be at its worst in Ethiopia, meteorologists were reporting that shifting weather patterns, part cyclical, part man-made, were changing the lives of entire tribes of people.

Some experts suggested the new weather patterns were quite possibly permanent. They reported that the Sahara Desert was expanding southward at a rate of three miles every year.[1] This resulted in a devastating famine that primarily swept across Northern Ethiopia gaining significant world attention. Footage on the evening news revealed a gruesome picture of suffering and death. Scattered everywhere were skeletal corpses, glassy-eyed children with swollen bellies, and weeping mothers who had few tears left to shed as entire households died.

But according to knowledgeable on-site researchers, the suffering was not caused mainly by a weather-induced famine. Nor was it even the neglect of the starving multitudes by the more prosperous nations such as the United Kingdom or the United States, who some suggested failed to respond more quickly to the suffering. Reporters bluntly asserted that the Ethiopians were starving by the tens of thousands because the then government of Ethiopia was Marxist. For political purposes the government wanted certain rebellious regions, primarily Tiger and Eritrea, to be prevented from receiving any humanitarian aid, according to the reporters.

A *Los Angeles Times* reporter stated:

> The people of Ethiopia — the several hundred thousand of them affected by drought and famine — are not suffering because of the neglect of the United States, the European Economic Community, or any other outside power. They are starving because of the neglect and the mismanagement of their own government.[2]

The writer further explained there is enough fertile soil in Ethiopia alone to feed not only their nation's more than fifty million inhabitants, but an additional three hundred million scattered throughout Africa. Political situations simply made it impossible to develop the land properly.

That same year, a massive fund-raising campaign featuring an array of the world's top entertainers was staged to raise money for the starving masses of Ethiopia. Labelled "U.S.A. for Africa," the rock concert raised a remarkable $46.1 million, targeted for those most needy regions — Eritrea and Tiger.

Two years later, when a full accounting of these funds emerged, it was determined that of the $46.1 million raised by "U.S.A. for Africa," only $80,000 of the total ever actually reached the most troubled regions, and none of those funds went for food. The $80,000 was used to establish a medical laboratory at a hospital in one of the troubled provinces.[3]

It wasn't that the fund-raisers intentionally misused the funds. Rather, the political climate was such within Ethiopia that none of the money could be earmarked for the starving people of Eritrea and Tiger. The massive funds were thus diverted to other needs in Africa. Something of a supernatural origin seemed to be holding a grip on the souls of men and women of the area. No matter how much compassion was manifested for the physical needs of the region, some unseen force kept the multitudes in need from receiving it.

Interestingly, that unexplained bondage to supernatural forces did not stop in the mid-1980s. Five years later, in April 1990, almost forty-five thousand metric tons of food were being off-loaded from ships at the Ethiopian port of Masada. They were completely destroyed by communist fighter pilots sent by the then Marxist government in Addis Ababa. It was food intended for those same hurting provinces.

Although the communist government is no longer in power in Ethiopia, this same general geographic region continues to be a picture of pain and poverty. Somalia, for example, is Ethiopia's immediate eastern neighbor where recent man-induced famine has affected millions, forcing the United Nations to take action.

Why this particular region? I recall listening to a journalist reporting from Ethiopia during the height of the 1984 crisis. According to his assessment, no matter what amount of resources might be released to alleviate the suffering, it probably wouldn't make too much difference in the years to come. "It is almost as if this region is cursed," he said, "and no matter what happens in our attempts to heal the suffering, the suffering will go on and perhaps become worse. It is as if the curses here come in cycles every few years."

Not long after that reporter shared his observations, the drought in the region was broken, and heavy rains fell. But even as many rejoiced in this long hoped-for miracle, it was soon discovered that the much needed rains actually opened the door for still another curse. According to an August 1986 *Time* magazine report:

> Last year, when heavy rains ended the worst drought in recent African history, the world heaved a collective sigh of relief. Hundreds of thousands of people had died of starvation, but the worst was over. Or so it seemed. The very rainstorms that broke the famine helped spawn another biblical curse on the blighted continent. The soggy soil nurtured locust eggs that had been lying dormant during the long dry spell. The eggs of four major species of locusts — brown, red, desert and migratory — and other grasshoppers are now hatching simultaneously across a great swath of the continent, from Mauritania to Ethiopia, down through Central Africa and into South Africa. According to officials at the U.S. Agency for International Development, Africa could be facing the worst locust plague in more than half a century.[4]

In even more recent months Sudan, Ethiopia's neighbor to the west, has taken a front row in this cycle of death. An article in *The Denver Post* explained:

> What is happening in Sudan may already have eclipsed the death tolls of other standard-bearers of misery, Somalia and the Balkans. Here it could become much, much worse.[5]

The reporter adds:

> A conspiracy of both nature and man gives birth to the misery here. Two years of hard rains in the south

drowned cattle and washed away crops. The civil war blocked trade or assistance from the north.[6]

Could this issue be entirely spiritual? Could it be that until certain unseen controlling demonic forces governing these regions are broken, these apparent cyclical curses will continue? Veteran missionaries who have faced these warfare realities for generations have come to grips with the supernatural nature of the battlefield.

Consider, for example, the unusual testimony of Ralph Mahoney, founder of World MAP. Mahoney tells an interesting story about a missionary friend who was engaging in literature distribution years ago in a small town on the international border between Uruguay and Brazil.[7] At the time of the incident, Brazil was experiencing a rather significant spiritual awakening. Churches were growing substantially, and many new fellowships were being established.

Uruguay, however, was experiencing just the opposite. How could one explain the fact that, on one side of the border, waves of spiritual victories seemed to flow in abundance, while merely stepping across the border brought that same person into a land of spiritual void? Interestingly, the specific international border where this worker labored ran directly down the main street of the town. Simply to cross the street meant you were in another country. Because it was not a large city, no immigration or customs formalities were required of the area's inhabitants who wished to move freely from one side of the street to another.

The missionary-evangelist began to notice a most unusual pattern as he distributed literature. Whenever he offered a gospel message to someone on the Brazil side of the street, they readily received it — often with a smile, frequently followed by a willingness to engage in a conversation regarding the content. However, when the worker merely crossed the street into Uruguayan territory, virtually no one wanted to receive the message.

Then a rather interesting thing occurred. For several minutes, the evangelist had been attempting to distribute messages on the Uruguayan side of the border with no success when he noticed that a woman who had angrily rejected his messages had just crossed the street. She apparently wanted to do some shopping on the Brazil side of the border. He crossed the street, keeping a careful eye on the woman's every movement. Slowly he approached her as she walked from shop to shop and again offered her the exact same literature she had rejected only moments earlier. This time, she received it joyfully.

Was this but another of those mere coincidences, or was there an invisible spiritual dynamic at work? Ralph Mahoney and others suggest[8] that Satan appears to control various regions of the world through a highly organized hierarchy that works collectively to cover these regions with spiritual darkness. Perhaps Isaiah 25:7 provides evidence. Here the prophet refers to "the covering cast over all the people, and the veil that is spread over all nations." Ezekiel adds insight in describing Satan as "the anointed cherub who covers" (Ezek. 28:14).

One thing is certain in the battle for the souls of humankind. It is a war of the invisible, and the conflict is intensifying. Writing in *Breaking the Strongholds in Your City,* George Otis Jr. cautions:

> The church of Jesus Christ must not shrink back from taking a long, hard look at the spiritual obstacles that stand between it and fulfillment of the Great Commission. The spiritual battlefield of the 1990s is increasingly becoming a supernatural place. There are those whose personal theology is resistant to this idea, but these are often untraveled western theoreticians who have yet to put their assumptions to the test of reality. By contrast, the vast majority of today's international pastors, missionaries, evangelists and intercessors have no need to be convinced that something is out there, and this "something" is manifesting itself in our material world.[9]

FIVE

PENETRATING THE DARKNESS

Seven Steps to
Victory-Assured Warfare

TO UNDERSTAND the believer's overall warfare we must recognize the nature of its outcome. We are clearly fighting from a position of victory. We are engaged in what might be termed victory-assured warfare. But when it comes to moving into such dark situations through prayer, how do we proceed?

Several years ago I was invited to speak to a group of short-term missionaries who were preparing to go into some of the more difficult regions of the world. My topic concerned the developing of a strategy for engaging in prayer warfare as it related to such regions. As I reflected prayerfully on the topic, it occurred to me that I really did not have, nor had I heard of, a particular step-by-step strategy for penetrating the darkness. It seemed that much had been said generally on the subject, but little specifically. There was considerable theory but not much practice. How, I thought, would one go about invading the invisible through prayer?

As I focused on the subject, asking God to reveal a biblical strategy for penetrating the darkness, insights began to flow from God's Word. Seven steps emerged that I believe provide at least a reasonable basis to begin.

1. Enter With Praise

Recognizing that praise enthrones God in a situation (Ps. 22:3), I realized that, to penetrate the spiritual darkness about us, we must first *enter with praise.* It's the believer's safest entryway into the invisible.

When the psalmist expressed that God is "enthroned in the praises of Israel" [His people] (Ps. 22:2-3), he was sharing a very foundational fact about the fruit of praise. Out of a climate of praise comes the enthroning of God. The original Hebrew word translated "inhabits" in some earlier translations ("thou that inhabitest the praises of Israel," KJV) comes from a root word in the Hebrew language meaning simply "to sit." Of course, where God sits we know to be His throne, hence the alternate translation: "God is enthroned upon [or amid] the praises of His people."

The psalmist elsewhere showed us quite clearly how we are to enter the Lord's presence. He said, "Enter into His gates with thanksgiving, and into His courts with praise" (Ps. 100:4). It would therefore seem logical that if we are to move into a position involving throne-room prayer activity — the place from which we will participate with our Lord by His Holy Spirit in casting down strongholds — we would need to do so through the vehicle of praise.

Indeed, the Scriptures often link praise with victorious warfare. The psalmist described this linkage when he wrote:

Let the saints be joyful in glory; let them sing aloud on their beds. Let the high praises of God be in their mouth, and a two-edged sword in their hand (Ps. 149:5-6).

Praise here is clearly a part of the battle.

Praise was also essential to the positioning of Judah's army for a humanly impossible victory during King Jehoshaphat's reign (2 Chr. 20). Here we read of Judah's lopsided confrontation with Moab, Ammon and Edom (2 Chr. 20:1-4).

As the lesson unfolds, it becomes obvious that God's people were facing a coalition of forces far beyond their capacity for victory. But a word from the Lord promptly came through the prophet Jahaziel explaining that God was going to fight Judah's battle. Judah needed only to take up a position as if they were going to fight. The Lord said simply, "Position yourselves" for the battle. Another translation declares, "Take up your positions" (NIV).

It appears that Jehoshaphat and his fellow warriors interpreted this to mean "position yourselves in a posture of praise." Scripture states:

> And when he [Jehoshaphat] had consulted with the people, he appointed those who should sing to the Lord, and who should praise the beauty of holiness, as they went out before the army and were saying: "Praise the Lord, for His mercy endures forever" (2 Chr. 20:21).

Significant to the account is the fact that neither the king nor his leaders specifically asked God to explain what He meant by "position yourselves." Instead, they consulted with one another, and the result was the appointment of worshippers to sing and offer praise over the battle. And the rest is a matter of biblical record.

> Now when they began to sing and to praise, the Lord set ambushes against the people of Ammon, Moab, and Mount Seir, who had come against Judah; and they were defeated (2 Chr. 20:22).

The relation of praise to victorious warfare is not merely an Old Testament phenomenon. When Paul and Silas occupied a prison cell at Philippi, it was a season of praise and worship that preceded their miraculous escape. The Bible says:

> But at midnight Paul and Silas were praying and singing hymns to God, and the prisoners were listening to them (Acts 16:25).

What happened next is one of the powerful "suddenlies" of Scripture.

> Suddenly there was a great earthquake, so that the foun-
> dations of the prison were shaken; and immediately all
> the doors were opened and everyone's chains were
> loosed (Acts 16:26).

Praise again provides the release point of still another power encounter resulting in victorious warfare.

How might we apply this first step in our strategic plan for penetrating the darkness? *We must exalt the Lord over the specific focus that represents the primary issue of our warfare prayer.* This is to suggest we approach all spiritual battles with concentrated praise and worship. And as the battle continues, we constantly sustain our praises amid our petitions and prayers of intercession regarding the situation.

Through praise, we are bringing all of God's nature and character to bear upon the darkness before us as we pray. We are enthroning God, through praise, in the circumstance being addressed in prayer. Most important, we are not focusing on how much control Satan has of a particular region or situation, but how much greater are the awesome power and authority of God over it. Praise dethrones Satan merely by enthroning God! Praise thus is the first step to penetrating the darkness.

2. Explore the Territory

Once we have enthroned God in our praises, which brings us into alignment with His throne-room purposes, we are ready to receive further directions regarding the spiritual battles before us. It is time to *explore the territory.* No commander would ever launch an attack into an area of conflict without first having scouts or intelligence officers explore the territory to be penetrated.

Jesus seemed to suggest something of this need to "observe" enemy activity within the context of prayer when He said, "Watch and pray" (Matt. 26:41). Our Lord was not only suggesting we must pray, but we must include a spirit of holy alertness in our praying.

Paul similarly told the Colossian believers, "Continue in prayer, and watch in the same with thanksgiving" (Col. 4:2, KJV). Another

56

translation suggests, "Devote yourselves to prayer, being watchful and thankful" (NIV).

Note also the process employed by Moses when he sent out the spies to explore the territory God had promised Israel (see Num. 13:2,18). Moses commands his warriors to "explore the land" (v. 2, NIV). Next he admonishes them to "see what the land is like and whether the people who live there are strong or weak, few or many" (v. 18, NIV).

Each of these directives concerns exploring territory ready to be taken. Generations earlier, God had said to Abraham, "Arise, walk in the land through its length and its width, for I give it to you" (Gen. 13:17).

It is clear that something was being released by Abraham's simply stepping out and exploring the territory God had promised him.

Such ancient acts often help us in clarifying biblical principles regarding our ongoing warfare. Supernatural vision to understand the darkness is especially essential to exploring the territory concerning warfare prayer for the nations. Jonathan Swift, author of *Gulliver's Travels,* reportedly once explained, "Vision is the art of seeing things invisible." To explore the territory in our preparation for prayer is to see things invisible.

How do we accomplish this, specifically, in our emerging strategy to penetrate the darkness? Simply stated, we must examine carefully the region (or situation) that has become the focus for our warfare praying. We need to survey that territory (or circumstance) in a general overview. This involves the gathering of facts related to the area of need.

Intercessors are increasingly recognizing the value of research as it relates to intelligent praying. We not only move into a region or situation to "pray about it," but we must maintain that watchful attitude as we pray. To do this, we must survey the situation carefully, seeking God's guidance concerning the focus of our intercession. Only then are we ready for our next vital step to penetrating the darkness.

3. Expose the Stronghold

Our prayerful explorations of the territory targeted for our prayers should lead us ultimately to *expose the strongholds* or spiritual forces ruling that region.

Consider Daniel's experience involving the prince of Persia (see Dan. 10:1-13). Here we discover something of a warfare encounter that exposes a stronghold. Even more, it reveals a high-level, ruling spiritual authority who appears to control a vast geographic area.

Daniel had been fasting and praying for several weeks before he actually received a visible response to his many days of prayer. However, when a particular angel finally arrived on the scene bringing Daniel's answer, we learn that a battle actually had ensued in the heavenlies for some twenty days.

> Then he said to me, "Do not fear, Daniel, for from the first day that you set your heart to understand, and to humble yourself before your God, your words were heard; and I have come because of your words" (Dan. 10:12).

The arriving angel explained that he had been hindered in the heavenlies by the "prince of the kingdom of Persia." From the Hebrew word *sar,* "prince" also might be translated "chief ruler." The angel then informed Daniel that his arrival might never have happened were it not for Michael, one of God's high-level spiritual princes, who came to assist the angelic messenger.

The Living Bible provides a most interesting paraphrase of this encounter:

> Then he [the angel] said, "Don't be frightened, Daniel, for your request has been heard in heaven and was answered the very first day you began to fast before the Lord and pray for understanding; that very day I was sent here to meet you. But for twenty-one days the mighty Evil Spirit who overrules the kingdom of Persia blocked my way. Then Michael, one of the top officers of the heavenly army, came to help me, so that I was able to break through these spirit rulers of Persia" (Dan. 10:12-13).

It is clear from this account that angelic activity may well be involved in response to the prayers of God's people, especially as it relates to strategic situations. Even after the angel concluded his visit with Daniel, he expressed a certain measure of concern regarding his return to his place of origination.

When I leave, I will go again to fight my way back, past the prince of Persia; and after him, the prince of Greece. Only Michael, the angel who guards your people Israel, will be there to help me (Dan. 10:20-21, TLB).

Again, we see this angel counting on Michael, a top-level heavenly warrior who appeared to have much greater authority in the region, to guide him through this supernatural no-man's land.

It is true that these passages are open to considerable theological debate, but we also recognize that something of a supernatural reality is described in such passages. Spiritual entities do appear to rule over territories — in this case, Greece and Persia (the latter representing modern Iran and Iraq), which are mentioned very specifically in this Daniel passage.

Some might question if there is any added potential to our praying if we are able to identify such forces. A few would suggest that more intelligent praying, which is made possible by accurate information, leads to a greater faith, thus producing a much more substantial result. In a later chapter on strategic-level prayer, some of these issues will be dealt with more directly, including a fuller explanation of the term *stronghold* as it relates to our warfare. For now, we simply need to acknowledge that principalities and powers rule in the heavenlies and must be dealt with if we are to evangelize lost souls in these regions.

Jesus said:

- No one can enter a strong man's house and plunder his goods, unless he first binds the strong man. And then he will plunder his house (Mark 3:27).

If Satan is to be equated in any sense to the strong man here, there can be no question as to what the "goods" represent. Satan's greatest treasure surely represents the souls of humankind. Thus, to snatch lost souls out of his grasp — that is, to spoil his goods — something of a spiritual "binding" must first take place. Demonic powers controlling regions must be dealt with boldly and directly.

Of course, no matter what conclusions we reach regarding the potential identifying of these invisible powers, one thing appears clear. Our enemy does have supernatural forces at work (Eph.

6:12), and something of an added dimension of faith and authority appears to accompany our praying when we are able to expose their strongholds.

But how do we accomplish this? Praying carefully over any research that was started during our previous warfare step (exploring the territory) is usually the place to begin in exposing a specific stronghold. It is one thing to research and study characteristics of a nation, people group or even geographic region. But it is often an entirely different matter to interpret these facts meaningfully, especially in order to enrich our prayer and evangelism strategies regarding a particular region or focus. Here we must rely on the Holy Spirit to speak clearly to us revealing what these facts mean.

As this process unfolds, we ought not to be surprised when details are given to help us pray more intelligently and boldly. When Paul instructed Ephesian believers on the subject of their ongoing spiritual warfare, he made it clear that their wrestling was not with flesh and blood but against a variety of invisible powers and ruling entities in some kind of ordered structure (see Eph. 6:12). Because wrestling involves a face-to-face assault including a hands-on, direct confrontation, we shouldn't think it strange at all that on occasion God may reveal the specific force or entity we are battling. Although it is invisible, it need not be unidentifiable. To expose such strongholds and the "strongmen" who occupy them prepares us for the steps of actual battle that follow.

4. Employ God's Word

At the heart of victorious warfare is the employment of God's Word in our praying. What is it to *employ God's Word* in our warfare prayer? When Paul spoke to Ephesian believers regarding preparation for spiritual battle, he described the totality of armor that was necessary to engage in battle: "Take unto you the whole armor of God" (Eph. 6:11, KJV). He knew only proper preparation could assure ultimate victory. After describing a variety of aspects of that armor, Paul then challenged believers to "take...the sword of the Spirit, which is the word of God" (Eph. 6:17).

It is not without significance that the last aspect of God's armor is His Word. Further, God's Word happens to be the only aspect of the armor that is not an analogy. All other aspects of the armor are "types" or examples. The helmet of salvation, for example, cannot be taken into our physical hands and placed upon our heads except perhaps in a childlike manner of going through the motions. Neither can we reach for an actual shield of faith. True, our faith is *like* a shield, but we can't touch it physically. These are spiritual qualities that comprise our invisible armor. The Word of God, however, is unique to the armor in that we can indeed touch it with our hands and see it with our eyes. It also happens to be the principal weapon of our warfare.

When Jesus confronted Satan in the wilderness (Luke 4:1-12), His primary weapon was the frequently repeated phrase "It is written" followed by just the right "word" from the Scriptures. Christ Himself thus used the Word to wage His spiritual battles.

Generations earlier Jeremiah recorded these words of the Lord:

> Is not my word like as a fire? saith the Lord; and like a hammer that breaketh the rock in pieces? (Jer. 23:29, KJV).

Again, we see the Word pictured as a weapon.

The author of Hebrews would speak in similar terms generations later.

> For the word of God is living and powerful, and sharper than any two-edged sword, piercing even to the division of soul and spirit (Heb. 4:12).

In his timeless hymn *A Mighty Fortress Is Our God,* Martin Luther devotes a stanza to the authority of God's Word:

> And though this world, with devils filled,
> Should threaten to undo us:
> We will not fear, for God hath willed
> His truth to triumph through us.
> The prince of darkness grim,
> We tremble not for him;
> His rage we can endure,
> For, lo! his doom is sure,
> One little word shall fell him!

How, then, might we employ God's Word in our prayer warfare against the darkness? First, we need to *establish a scriptural plan of assault* for confronting a specific stronghold. For this to happen, we must live in the Word on a daily basis. Remember that Jesus was only able to say, "It is written," and declare just the right portion of Scripture necessary to repel an enemy attack because somewhere in his early years he stored up the Word in His heart. Simply stated, He had done His homework.

We, too, must digest the Word, discern its proper application and then direct it toward the target. Faith giants of earlier generations like George Müller, Charles Spurgeon and David Brainerd would often refer to this kind of entreaty as "praying God's Word" or "pleading His promises." They had learned that employing a word from God in prayer was the same as saying to Satan, "This is what God says about this matter, and if you have any problems with this you can take it up with Him!"

5. Enlist Angelic Help

As mentioned earlier, angels become involved significantly in response to the prayers of God's people. Thus, the next step in penetrating the darkness is to *enlist angelic help.* But here we need a vital point of clarification. *To suggest that we enlist angelic help is not to say that we are to pray to angels.* It is, however, to suggest that we have a biblical authority to expect angels to come into our battle as the result of our prayers.

Indeed, the psalmist, on at least one occasion, prayed for the release of an angel into a very specific conflict.

> Let those be put to shame and brought to dishonor who seek after my life;...And let the angel of the Lord chase them (Ps. 35:4-5).

This would suggest we are in order to go to God in prayer, enlisting angelic assistance for our battles.

The Hebrew word for angel is *mal'ak* which is translated "to dispatch as a deputy." Angels literally are dispatched by the Lord into a variety of situations, often in response to our prayers. In the beloved ninety-first psalm, verse 11, we read:

For he shall give His angels charge over you, to keep you in all your ways.

The author of Hebrews explains further that angels are "sent out to render service for the sake of those who will inherit salvation" (Heb. 1:14, NAS).

In one interesting Old Testament passage, 1 Kings 22:18-22, we read how God is surrounded by "the host of heaven" (still another expression describing angels) when He calls for one of them to persuade evil King Ahab to go into a battle that will lead to his total destruction. One of the host responds by saying, "I will persuade him."

God asks that angel, "In what way?"

The angel answers, "I will go out and be a lying spirit in the mouth of all his prophets."

In another case, King Hezekiah had received an evil letter of condemnation from his enemy, King Sennacherib. He then spread it before the Lord (Is. 37:14). God answered by sending an angel in a single evening who destroyed 185,000 Assyrian troops (Is. 37:36). Here again we see clear evidence that, in response to believing prayer, angels are often sent into a spiritual battle.

The seven angels of Revelation 8:1-2, who are commissioned to sound trumpets in the end-time scenario, are not permitted to do so until the prayers of the saints are released at the altar (Rev. 8:1-6). Then, when the seventh angel finally sounds his trumpet, the kingdoms of the world instantly become the kingdoms of Christ. Again we see the relationship of prayer to the dispatching of angels to perform their heavenly functions. The Daniel lesson also cited earlier (Dan. 10:1-13) proves this point.

How do we enlist angelic help through warfare prayer? We must exercise our right as an heir of God and joint heir of Christ (Rom. 8:17), who is entitled to angelic assistance. Indeed, if Jesus can enlist angelic participation, dispatching angels for battle, we ought to link up with Him as His joint heirs in this angelic release.

6. Enforce Calvary's Victory

All of this seems to flow naturally into our next step for penetrating the darkness. We must *enforce Calvary's victory.*

In *Destined for the Throne,* the late Paul E. Billheimer wrote:

> Prayer is not begging God to do something which He is unwilling to do. It is not overcoming reluctance in God. It is enforcing Christ's victory over Satan. It is implementing upon earth heaven's decisions concerning the affairs of men. Calvary legally destroyed Satan and canceled all of his claims. God placed the enforcement of Calvary's victory in the hands of the church as proven by Matthew 18:18 and Luke 10:17-19. He has given to her the "power of attorney." She is His "deputy." But this delegated authority is wholly inoperative apart from the prayers of a believing church.[1]

Consider Christ's words to the apostle Peter:

> I will give you the keys of the kingdom of heaven; whatever you bind on earth will be bound in heaven, and whatever you loose on earth will be loosed in heaven (Matt. 16:19, NIV).

Two chapters later in Matthew 18:18, we notice Christ repeating these words, adding further evidence that this wasn't merely a promise given to a single disciple, Peter. All of Christ's disciples share in this authority to confront spiritual forces that hinder God's plans and purposes.

As mentioned in an earlier chapter, when we read the account of Satan being removed finally from the heavenlies (Rev. 12:7-11), it appears evident that the saints on earth are the ones who employ "the blood of the Lamb" and "the word of their testimony," making possible an angel-led victory in the heavenlies. The overcoming power didn't come directly from the angels as much as from the capacity of the angels to win this warfare because the saints were enforcing Calvary's victory. Again we remind ourselves that *none* of this Revelation miracle happened until first the vials of prayer, filled with the prayers of the saints, were released at the throne of God (Rev. 8:3-6).

How do we enforce Calvary's victory as we penetrate the darkness? We must invoke the power of the cross and the blood of Jesus *verbally* in our prayers, focusing that authority on barriers the enemy has set up as obstacles to the fulfillment of God's purposes. We must command with authority, confront strongholds directly and claim the blood of the Lamb and the power of Jesus' name as the foundational basis for our praying.

7. Eliminate the Stronghold

The final step in our confrontation with the darkness is to *eliminate the stronghold.* This, of course, only the Holy Spirit can accomplish. Therefore we must move into a heightened sense of Holy Spirit dependence as we seek the literal elimination of a stronghold. Believers of previous generations often referred to this as "praying through" regarding a circumstance or issue. This simply meant they persisted in prayer until the Holy Spirit gave "witness" that a victory had come.

Of course, in practical terms, if a stronghold controlling a region is eliminated, immediate results should accompany the absence of that force. For example, if a stronghold of apathy and rejection of the gospel has long gripped a geographic region and there's a sudden witness that this grip has been broken, it should be relatively easy to test the victory. Simply go again with the gospel to the region where the rejection was strongest and see if there's a greater receptivity. Our earlier example among the mountain Kwaio of the Solomon Islands proves this point.

Keep in mind that eliminating a stronghold is something we are dealing with here in spiritual terms, not in a physical sense, even though what we do in the spiritual realm may impact the physical significantly. For example, we may view a pornographic bookstore in our community as a stronghold and greatly desire to eliminate it. Actually, a spirit of greed and lust giving place to the stronghold is most likely the real reason the stronghold exists. Thus, the actual solution to removing the stronghold may be not to "resist" the bookstore so much as to seek God for a revival of conviction and repentance to sweep through your community. Then the spirit of greed and lust will be removed from the hearts of those who own that bookstore as well as those who frequent it.

This is not to suggest that we lack the authority to pray directly against obstacles that rise up to oppose God's purposes. Jesus told His disciples that they could command mountains to be moved

(Mark 11:22-24), a subject we will examine more carefully in a later chapter. When Christ used the analogy of "speaking" to a mountain, He certainly would have known that throughout ancient Israel mountains were often the places where pagan gods were worshipped. Thus, a mountain represented a concrete picture of an enemy stronghold. Jesus certainly knew of God's word to Isaiah:

> Behold, I will make you into a new threshing sledge with sharp teeth; you shall thresh the mountains and beat them small (Is. 41:15-16).

There is also significant biblical evidence that true revival praying can result in God's people going forth to make tangible social changes that cause the actual removal of physical strongholds. Such a case is seen in King Hezekiah's early years of reign (2 Chr. 29-31). Here a great revival results because of a nationwide spirit of repentance. Key to this awakening is the fact that the prayers of God's people rose to "His holy dwelling place, to heaven" (2 Chr. 30:27).

But we must not miss the very next verse (which actually falls in chapter 31). It reveals the results of this repentant, revival praying.

> Now when all this was finished [all the repentance and prayer], all Israel who were present went out to the cities of Judah and broke the sacred pillars in pieces, cut down the wooden images, and threw down the high places and the altars...until they had utterly destroyed them all (2 Chr. 31:1).

The direct result of all the prayer and repentance was a bold authority that came upon the people to put feet to their prayers. They went forth to impact their nation in a most tangible way.

Applied today, this would suggest that believers should become more actively involved in the outcome of their prayers. To pray against that pornographic bookstore may need to be followed up with a trip to a city council meeting where the pornographic shop is an agenda item. It is not to suggest we rent bulldozers to destroy the shop physically, thus violating our laws. It is, however, to become involved in the process that might bring practical change to our community.

One church in Northern California did just this. They put feet to their prayers by going into some of the most troubled areas of their community to hold block parties. They targeted areas where the sale of "crack" cocaine and other drugs had been rampant. They took music groups and food to minister love to the people. Each time they did this, the drug pushers would move out of that area. These teams would then move systematically to other drug-infested areas, taking this same message of loving concern. Their efforts became so successful that the local police department began calling upon this congregation to assist them in other areas. Simply stated, it worked. Believers had gone forth to break the strongholds of evil activity on their street corners and accomplished what local police had been unable to do.

What, then, is the key to eliminating strongholds? Aggressive warfare prayer is but a first step. We must then become involved in the process of replacing that demonic stronghold with a spiritual fortress that honors God. Take that pornographic bookstore again as an example. Imagine a Christian bookstore taking its place. Or picture a new church being planted in that very storefront. Could the enemy ever again claim that site for his evil intention?

The same principles apply to the breaking of strongholds hindering world evangelization. Several years ago powerful miracles took place throughout the old Soviet Union as the prayers of believers globally were marvelously answered. The stronghold of communism appeared totally broken. But suddenly we were faced with a chilling challenge. What would be built up in its place?

In the former Soviet republics of Central Asia, for example, it soon became evident that Islam might well rise up as a much greater stronghold than communism. Why? Because the church appeared unwilling to put feet to its prayers by releasing the needed resources to take advantage of this new freedom and evangelize these regions quickly.

Indeed, eliminating a stronghold necessitates putting something in its place that can stand forever against the enemy, preventing him from reestablishing his own stronghold in that same region. Regarding world evangelization, that "something" must include the saturation planting of churches by means of systematic evangelism strategies that provide access to the gospel by every person in a region. There simply is no other way.

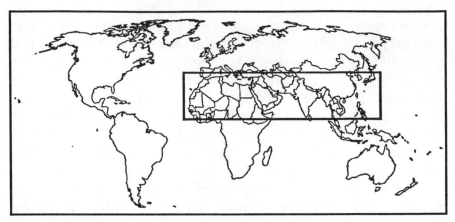

The 10/40 Window is a geographic region marked by the boundaries of 10 degrees north of the equator to 40 degrees north and stretching from the west coast of Africa to the eastern borders of China. First designated the 10/40 Window by missions strategist Luis Bush, the region is home to 97 percent of the peoples living in the world's least evangelized nations. But it has only 8 percent of the world's missionary force laboring among them. The 10/40 Window is also the headquarters of most of the world's non-Christian religions such as Islam, Hinduism and Buddhism.

Thus, our prayer strategy to penetrate the darkness in such demonically controlled regions as the 10/40 Window begins with the power of praise and continues with a bold employment of God's Word and the power of the cross. But it ends with a practical hands-on involvement in the harvest. We are reminded that God's commissioning of Jeremiah as a prophetic intercessor (a subject we'll look at more carefully later) didn't end merely with a call to "root out," "pull down," "destroy" and "throw down" enemy strongholds, but included the mandate to "build" and to "plant" (Jer. 1:10).

It is one thing to penetrate the darkness of a region through our passionate and persistent praying, but it's entirely another matter to establish a permanent life-giving source of light forever, preventing the darkness from reclaiming that area. We must penetrate the darkness for the purpose of eliminating it. Planting must accompany the praying.

"Evangelism without intercession is like an explosive without a detonator," German evangelist Reinhard Bonnke has wisely declared. But, he adds, "intercession without evangelism is like a detonator without an explosive."[2]

SIX

A VIEW TOWARD JERICHO

*The Joshua Call
for the Jericho Hour*

MORE THAN a generation had passed since the promise had been given by God to the nation of Israel that they were to receive a land flowing with milk and honey. Now it was time to possess that promise. But Joshua, Israel's leader, knew instinctively that obtaining the promise would not come without a fight. In fact, it would ultimately involve a series of battles and a good deal of bloodshed.

Imagine Joshua's concerns as he readied his army to attack their first major obstacle — the Canaanite fortress of Jericho. Today, when Christians refer to Jericho, various thoughts come to mind.

Most immediate would be the picture of towering walls crumbling miraculously as God intervenes. We also think of a huge Israeli army marching around the walls in silence for seven days. We've heard the story so often that it almost seems logical for God to have given His people such a strategy. Yet a careful look at the overall Jericho account reveals how unusually unique this strategy was. It also provides powerful insights into the nature of the spiritual conflict before us during this historic hour of the church's quest to evangelize the world in our generation. A view toward Jericho could indeed prove most beneficial.

The Jericho Vision

The Jericho lesson begins with a simple declaration, "And it came to pass, when Joshua was by Jericho, that he lifted up his eyes and looked" (Josh. 5:13, KJV).

Events preceding this critical moment had been most challenging. Joshua was finally experiencing the culmination of literally decades of simple obedience to the call of God.

Forty years earlier Joshua had been one of only two spies of twelve who had faithfully believed God. Joshua and Caleb alone were convinced that Israel was able to possess the land. But because the majority had voted contrary to the promise of God, Israel was doomed by its unbelief to forty years of wilderness wandering.

Now Joshua is about to witness the final fulfillment of faith in that promise. Because the time of day is described as being past twilight, one might assume Joshua had chosen the very early morning hours to conduct this survey. We assume he is alone as the context refers to no other Israelis present. The Bible simply says, "He lifted up his eyes and looked."

Here, almost hidden in the text, we discover one of the first keys to understanding the nature of spiritual conflict. *We must take time to look.* Critical to victorious warfare is our ability to see into the unseen. As an anonymous writer once expressed, "Only those who see into the invisible will ever be able to attempt the impossible." Vision clearly is essential to victory.

When Elisha approached the senior prophet, Elijah, and requested of him a double portion of his spirit, Elijah made it clear that something first had to happen if he was to receive the miracle.

You have asked a hard thing. Nevertheless, if you see me
when I am taken from you, it shall be so for you; but if
not, it shall not be so (2 Kin. 2:10).

Elijah was simply suggesting, "If you can see into the invisible
when I am taken up, the miracle you have requested will happen."

Students of Scripture know well the outcome of this encounter.
Elisha's eyes were indeed opened as he saw Elijah carried into the
heavenlies. In that instant, Elijah's mantle fell, and the young warrior
seized it. He thus launched his own series of marvelous miracles that
didn't end until he had witnessed more than twice the number of
miracles the old prophet had recorded — a true double portion.

To see into the heavenlies is indeed a key to understanding the
nature of the battle before us. Joshua could never have begun to
approach the challenge of Jericho had he not first opened his eyes
and looked. True, he was looking at a physical fortress, but he was
likewise looking with the realization that God alone had a plan to
penetrate that fortress.

The Jericho Encounter

Important to understanding the heart of the Jericho lesson is
what Joshua actually saw as he stood alone gazing toward Jericho
(Josh. 5:13). In one instance, the Israeli leader was contemplating
the reality of this towering fortress, and the next, something radi-
cally altered his view. A presence had entered the picture.

A Man stood opposite him with His sword drawn in His
hands. And Joshua went to Him and said to Him, "Are
you for us or for our adversaries?" (Josh. 5:13b).

A careful examination of the text reveals this presence, who
identified Himself as "captain of the host of the Lord" (Josh. 5:14),
to be Christ Himself. This is but one of the several pre-incarnate
appearances of our Lord in Scripture. Scholars also believe it was
Christ who appeared to Abraham (Gen. 18) and later to Samson's
parents (Judg. 13:20). Theologians refer to these encounters as
"christophanies," an expression derived from the Greek words
Christos (meaning Christ) and *phaneros* (meaning manifestation).

These were literally manifestations of the eternal Christ prior to His physical birth in Bethlehem as recorded in the Gospels.

When Joshua initially encountered this glorified being he had no idea of what or whom he was seeing. He only saw what must have appeared to be a supernatural being with a sword in his hand. Immediately he inquired, "Are you for us or for our adversaries?"

The Lord's reply was most interesting: "Neither, but as commander of the army of the Lord I have now come" (Josh. 5:14, NIV). The Lord was suggesting that He hadn't come to join anyone's side, but rather He had come to take over command.

As Abraham Lincoln said during the Civil War when asked if God was on the side of the North or the South, "I am not so concerned as to whether or not God is on my side as I am concerned to know if I am on His."[1]

When Joshua heard Christ identify Himself as "commander of the army of the Lord," his reaction was instantaneous: "And Joshua fell on his face to the earth and worshiped" (Josh. 5:14). It was now clear that Joshua viewed this being as much more than a mere angel.

When viewing the victory at Jericho it is all too easy to think of the falling walls as the real miracle. Actually, the real miracle of Jericho was the fact that Jesus was there and that Joshua was wise enough to join *His* army. The rest of the miracle never would have happened had Joshua not encountered the Captain. It was, after all, the Captain who gave him the strategy, and without that strategy there could have been no victory.

Equally essential to understanding this encounter was Joshua's obedient response of removing his sandals in recognition that the ground he lay upon was holy (Josh. 5:15). The removing of Joshua's shoes was not only symbolic of his occupying holy ground but was also something of a surrendering back to the Lord of a powerful promise given to him earlier that wherever the soles of his shoes were to tread, the Lord would give it to him (see Josh. 1:3).

The removing of one's shoes in ancient Israel was a significant symbolic gesture picturing surrender. When we read of the experience of Ruth and Boaz (Ruth 4:7-8), during which Boaz redeemed the estate of the deceased kinsman Elimelech, Naomi's husband, we see this custom exercised.[2]

The Old Testament law provided for those occasions in which an inheritance that had been lost could be redeemed through a *kinsman-redeemer.* If a man, through poverty, was forced to mortgage his property and was later unable to meet the payment on the date of the maturity of the mortgage, the man holding the mortgage could keep the land until the year of Jubilee (which came every fifty years), at which time it reverted automatically to its former owner. But before this date, a kinsman-redeemer (the nearest male blood relation) could go into a civil court and, by payment, recover the land for his relative. If the relation had died without an heir, then it became the duty of the kinsman-redeemer to marry his widow and raise up the name of his "brother."

The story of Ruth and Boaz is the biblical example of this ancient custom. Boaz redeemed the estate of the deceased Elimelech, Naomi's husband, by marrying Ruth, the widow of one of Elimelech's sons. There was a kinsman closer in relation than Boaz, but he had chosen not to be the kinsman-redeemer.

This left the way open for Boaz, who was next in line. In completing the transaction, whereby the inheritance was redeemed and Ruth became his wife, an interesting old custom was observed. Scripture reads:

> (Now in earlier times in Israel, for the redemption and transfer of property to become final, one party took off his sandal and gave it to the other. This was the method of legalizing transactions in Israel.) So the kinsman-redeemer said to Boaz, "Buy it yourself." And he removed his sandal (Ruth 4:7-8, NIV).

The owner of the property then took off his sandal and surrendered it as evidence of completing his act of redemption.

This custom no doubt originated from the fact that the right to tread the soil of one's property belonged only to the owner of it, and therefore the transfer of a sandal was considered an appropriate representation of the transfer of property.

The fact that the Lord asked Joshua to take off his shoes may not only have meant that he now was occupying holy ground, but that he was being asked to surrender his own right to go in and possess the very land God had promised Israel. Perhaps the Lord was reminding Joshua that although He was giving him the land, He alone had the power to obtain the victory for Joshua.

The Jericho Strategy

Essential in our view toward Jericho is the fact that Joshua is still on his face when Christ reveals His strategy to conquer Jericho. Although Joshua 5 ends with Joshua prostrate before the Lord, and chapter 6 begins with a description of Jericho as a fortified city, the chapter placement is unfortunate because it suggests the passing of time. Actually, Joshua is still on his face receiving instructions from the Lord as chapter 6 begins.

This adds vital significance to our lesson. After Joshua had asked his Commander, "What message does my Lord have for his servant?" (Josh. 5:14, NIV), the Lord responds by asking Joshua to remove his sandals. He goes on (in chapter 6) to reveal the Jericho strategy immediately. All the while Joshua is still on his face, a reminder to us that God's best strategies most often come to those willing to humble themselves in prayer, even prostrate, before the Lord.

Note specifically the uniqueness of the overall strategy given to Joshua as he waits prayerfully before his Captain.

First, the strategy is clearly *spiritual*. In other words, there was no tactical military significance to the strategy. Indeed, had the Lord told Joshua to build several battering rams, take them to the gates of Jericho and begin hammering away, we could see some military value. However, simply to march around the city walls in total silence was militarily impractical. It was therefore clear that the victory would be won in the spiritual realm.

Second, we notice the strategy also involved the *physical*. Although God intended to intervene in His own miraculous way spiritually, He wanted His people to be involved physically. It was necessary for them to set their feet in motion and respond in obedience to His call for their participation in the miracle. Again, we are reminded of the many times in Scripture that our Lord called His prophets or leaders to step out physically as a first step toward seeing Him respond supernaturally (Josh. 3:8).

Third, the strategy was *radical*. Today we look at the Jericho plan as if it were the normal thing to do. However, we must not forget how unusual the strategy must have seemed at the time. No attack had ever been carried out quite like this. Israel's army was to walk around Jericho's walls in total silence once daily for six days and then seven times on the seventh day. It has been suggested that God may have required Israel to walk for a week in absolute silence because He was tired of their forty years of murmuring in the wilderness. He didn't want to run the risk of His people further limiting His capacity to act on their behalf through their faithless complaining.

Next, we note that the strategy was *simple*. Israel's army had only to go on several rather long walks in order to obey the Lord's directive. There was nothing complex about it. Anyone who could walk could be involved in fulfilling the plan. So it is with prayer. Anybody can pray.

Then we notice the strategy was *inexpensive*. No costly weapons were required to accomplish this God-given plan. In fact, all that actually was needed were seven rams' horns. This is typical of God's strategies which are usually very simple and generally quite inexpensive. All that was required for Israel to obey the Lord's directive for taking Jericho was to put feet to their obedience. The only cost incurred would have been food for their people during the seven-day campaign.

Finally, the strategy was *focused*. Israel was to concentrate on just one specific stronghold — Jericho. In fact, the Jericho strategy was not repeated for any of the other cities that were eventually taken, a reminder to us of our need to seek God for each new challenge set before us. Like Israel, we also can rely upon God to remove each obstacle standing in the way of His purposes as we trust Him. One obstacle at a time will be conquered. As Moses testified of their earlier campaigns: "There was not one city too strong for us; the Lord our God delivered all to us" (Deut. 2:36).

The Jericho Victory

Our view toward Jericho also reminds us that no wall or obstacle Satan has erected ever can be removed by human methods. The Jericho narrative tells us that when Israel carefully obeyed the Lord's simple directive, "the wall fell down flat" (Josh. 6:20). Only God can remove Jericho walls. We are simply workers together with Him in fulfilling whatever plan He has revealed to us.

But central to this lesson is our recognition that although God's supernatural intervention is critical to our victory, the totality of that victory is predicated on our partnering with God to bring it to fruition.

The miracle among the mountainous Kwaio in the Solomon Islands required God's absolute intervention. However, the fruits of harvest did not begin to grow until there first was a prolonged period of fasting and prayer followed by a courageous trek by obedient workers into this dark region.

Israel's victory at this ancient fortress called Jericho resulted not merely from the miraculous falling of the walls, but from the aggressive seizing of the city by God's people who obediently responded to the miracle.

Of the city's capture, the Bible says:

> Then the people went up into the city, every man straight before him, and they took the city (Josh. 6:20).

God removes walls, but He doesn't seize cities. He may likewise remove barriers that keep people from having access to the gospel, but He will not evangelize them.

Rees Howells, one of the twentieth century's most remarkable intercessors, often spoke of our need as intercessors to become a part of the answer to our own prayers. Howells would remind his students in Swansea, Wales, during World War II that it was not good enough to pray that God would thrust forth workers if we were unwilling to be counted among the "thrusted"!* Said in the context of the Jericho lesson, if we surrender our sandals to Jesus in prayer, it shouldn't surprise us if He hands them back to us with a directive — "Now go and evangelize!"

The Jericho Model

God still has a plan to remove Jericho-type walls that keep His purposes from being realized throughout the world. Encouraging indicators suggest that God is preparing His people for a new assault on every remaining barrier. It seems that a corporate Jericho vision is being given to the church, something that has touched our ministry, Every Home for Christ, in a most practical way.

---

* I highly recommend that the reader obtain a copy of *Rees Howells: Intercessor* by Norman Grubb (Fort Washington, Pa.: Christian Literature Crusade, 1979) to read the entire story of Rees Howells.

Several years ago, the leadership of EHC felt led to pray about its physical location as a ministry. Little did we realize the implications of those prayers. It seemed the Lord was directing the ministry to move to a location where it might function better in carrying out its overall vision, especially in relation to other like-minded ministries. After we had prayerfully discussed the matter at length, it was felt the Lord was leading the ministry to relocate from Southern California to Colorado Springs, Colorado. At first, most of the discussion centered on the ministry's functioning in a place that might prove to be more economical, thus allowing us to make better use of our limited resources.

However, as we continued praying, it became obvious that God had much more in mind. We soon discovered that more than thirty other evangelical ministries had already located in the community, a number that was to surpass fifty within eighteen months of our eventual relocation. Interestingly, many of these organizations had mission statements related to some aspect of evangelizing the least-evangelized regions of the world.

As we sought God regarding our relocation, it became clear that we were moving into a new position of promise not unlike that experienced by ancient Israel. The Jericho picture became instrumental in the transition. Our move was to make possible the ultimate fulfillment of the vision statement of Every Home for Christ which speaks of working with all of Christ's body to help take a clear presentation of the gospel of Jesus Christ to every home on earth. But like Joshua and his forces, we recognized that Jericho-type walls stood as a formidable barrier in many regions of the world that, quite simply, made it impossible to fulfill our ministry objectives. We realized the same had to be true of many related ministries, some of whom were being drawn uniquely to the very same community.

Was God indeed speaking to us in all of this? We concluded He was. Soon a beautiful picture emerged of what might happen if many of these ministries were to link together, some even under the same roof, through a strategic center for prayer and evangelism. The center would focus its combined spiritual energies primarily on the most-difficult-to-evangelize regions of the world, like the 10/40 Window.

Incorporating the Jericho picture, the facility would be called the Jericho Center. It would ultimately house numerous ministries that might share combined resources. These resources would help each of the ministries, although operating as separate entities, serve one another to see these most troubled regions of the world penetrated with the gospel. At the heart of the center would be a continuous covering of prayer, made possible by trained teams of three to six intercessors who would be responsible for two- or three-hour prayer shifts either once a week or once a month. Because these teams would be composed of a variety of believers from different churches and ministries, they would actually form what might be called a continuing "concert of prayer" for the nations.

Several of the resident ministries would represent catalyst-type networking strategies for world evangelism as well as church planting. Therefore it became apparent that much of this prayer would help cover the numerous strategic consultations and planning conferences that might take place at this center on a rather regular basis.

The vision was growing in clarity. All strategic planning conducted at the center, including board meetings and planning sessions of individual resident ministries, as well as corporate planning sessions, would be covered from start to finish by trained intercessors. At least two or three of the resident organizations would be prayer mobilization ministries physically present to assist in the managing of the prayer focus of the center. No one ministry would do it all. We were catching a vision of what might happen if ongoing strategic-level prayer were linked continuously to systematic plans for global world evangelization. It was becoming exciting indeed.

Within days of our ministry's arrival in Colorado Springs, I shared some of this unique picture with two pastors of the city who were deeply committed to intercessory prayer. Their eyes lit up as they began explaining to me what numerous local intercessors had referred to for years as a coming spiritual NORAD to Colorado Springs that would ultimately touch the nations of the world.

NORAD, an acronym for North American Aerospace Defense Command, is a well-known Colorado Springs landmark located in the towering Cheyenne Mountains at the southern boundary of the city. For decades, NORAD, a sophisticated military installation carved out of thousands of tons of granite, has been America's primary means for tracking strategic enemy missile activity globally.

During the Persian Gulf War, for example, when Iraqi troops launched Scud missiles at Israel, NORAD knew instantly every detail about each launching, including where it came from and precisely where it was heading. Instantaneous communications were radioed to U.S. Patriot missile batteries that took immediate and decisive action. NORAD, though thousands of miles away, was essential to victory on the battlefield.

God had given detailed insights regarding the Jericho Center, including the fact that He intended to use this center to link many thousands of teams of intercessors together globally with a similar focus. Only after that did we realize that a prophetic word had come years earlier to different groups of local intercessors that a spiritual NORAD would someday come to this city.

But, for us, the frosting on the spiritual cake regarding this unique picture came when Every Home for Christ's vice president of ministries, Brad Fallentine, first heard of the NORAD vision. (Brad had been given the assignment of providing initial management of the Jericho Center as it unfolds.) Tears were impossible for Brad to contain as details of the NORAD vision were shared with our staff by a local pastor who had heard this unusual "word" long before Every Home for Christ ever contemplated relocating to Colorado Springs.

Brad's tears were certainly understandable. Prior to his joining the staff of Every Home for Christ, he had worked for several years in the area of strategic computer programming with the System Development Corporation of Santa Monica, California. One of their primary clients was NORAD. Brad, who now was going to help establish a spiritual NORAD, had literally helped design the computer programming that enabled the physical NORAD to test its capabilities globally through computerized scenarios of potential enemy attacks. What he had done in the physical realm years ago, before he had even become a committed Christian, would now be done in the supernatural realm at the Jericho Center in Colorado Springs. God had blessed us with still another of His divine "coincidences"! ⏳

SEVEN

EXTRAORDINARY PRAYER

*Mobilizing Special Forces
in the Battle for the Nations*

A S THE early hours of the Persian Gulf conflict unfolded, the Iraqi leader, Saddam Hussein, became convinced that an arsenal of America's battleships and aircraft carriers was launching an all-out assault against the beachhead of Kuwait City. Tens of thousands of Iraqi troops were put on alert, and many were diverted to the area. For hours the predawn sky was aglow with what appeared to be the streaks of incoming rockets. Artillery shells seemed to be exploding everywhere along the vulnerable coastline.

Iraqi troops guarding the vast inland border between Iraq and Saudi Arabia were diverted toward the shoreline. Unknowingly this allowed a broad opening for the unhindered entry of thousands of allied troops who were planning all along to flood into Iraq through a narrow backdoor corridor, far into the interior of the country.

Only later would it be learned that all of the explosions and apparent fire power along the Kuwaiti coast were not caused by an American fleet of warships and aircraft carriers. They were actually the result of but four highly trained "Navy Seals" (carefully trained seamen) who had worked for several long nights in two small rubber dingies planting a vast array of highly sophisticated underwater explosives. Each device was equipped with special timers that, when exploded in proper sequence, would give the incredible impression of an all-out attack of an entire fleet of ships storming the coastline.

Saddam Hussein had been fooled into committing thousands of Iraqi troops into a region American forces had no intention of attacking because of the effectiveness of four carefully trained "special forces" of Navy engineers who did exactly what they had been trained to do. The biblical injunction seemed to be working for the Allied troops — one can chase a thousand, and two can put ten thousand to flight (see Deut. 32:30).

A Call for Specialists

We are entering a season when it appears that God is bringing much greater clarity and intensity to the rapidly expanding global prayer movement. In the last ten years remarkable advances have taken place regarding concerted prayer for both spiritual awakening and world evangelization. Some of the largest prayer gatherings in history have taken place during these years. Several have united as many as fifty thousand or more believers to pray for cities and nations. Such would have been unthinkable even a decade ago.

But now it seems the Lord is raising up from within this vast movement much smaller bands of warriors who are becoming even more focused in their praying. They are engaging in what might be called strategic-level warfare, and these thousands of small groups, composed of quite ordinary believers, might do as much if not more damage to Satan's kingdom than any previous spiritual force in history.[1]

These believers appear to be coming to a new understanding of our weaponry and the fact that any committed believer truly can qualify for enlistment in these special forces. Paul made this clear when he spoke of both our warfare and our weaponry.

> It is true that I am an ordinary, weak human being, but I don't use human plans and methods to win my battles. I use God's mighty weapons, not those made by men, to knock down the devil's strongholds. These weapons can break down every proud argument against God and every wall that can be built to keep men from finding him (2 Cor. 10:3-5, TLB).

Although ordinary, weak human beings do appear to qualify, a basic understanding of prayer at a strategic level is certainly helpful.

What is strategic-level prayer? Some might define it simply as "warfare prayer," although all prayer, to some degree, involves spiritual warfare. This is true because whenever we pray our prayers can limit or hinder Satan or his agents at least to a degree. For example, a mother who prays for a child departing for school is, in a sense, raising up a shield of protection around that child through her prayers of intercession. To an extent, this may involve certain elements of warfare. But it might not be considered truly "strategic" in light of its potential impact upon either spiritual awakening in the church globally or the evangelization of the world.

Obviously, some matters for prayer do possess a greater significance when examined in the light of eternity. These we might call strategic. The "praying open" of a closed nation to the gospel, for example, is surely more eternally significant than the petitioning of God for the healing of an aching tooth, unless perhaps it's your toothache!

Strategic means that which counts the most. It also means something essential to the fulfilling of a plan or objective or something of greater value. When Every Home for Christ felt directed to relocate its international office from Southern California, several cities in America were considered. We quickly determined Colorado Springs to be especially strategic. Employing the word *strategic* meant our leadership felt this particular community was of greater value than other potential locations.

Level refers to a place or position of a person, object or concept in relation to another similar person, object or concept. As president of the international ministry of Every Home for Christ, I am on a different level from that of our various other directors. We use the word *level* to note the difference. In the general subject of mathematics, calculus is on a different level from algebra. Strategic-level prayer, then, is prayer that counts the most in confronting a higher level of spiritual forces ("principalities" and "powers," Eph. 6:10-12) that govern the affairs of men.

Levels of Warfare

C. Peter Wagner, professor of church growth at Fuller Theological Seminary in Pasadena, California, has been drawn more and more into the subject of prayer warfare in recent years. He has recognized that prayer plays a vital role in all truly successful evangelism and church growth strategies. Explaining that there are probably many discernible levels of spiritual warfare, Wagner suggests three generalized levels for which he feels there is a fairly broad consensus among Christian leaders specializing in this type of ministry.[2] They include:

1. *Ground-level spiritual warfare,* which according to Wagner, primarily concerns the ministry of casting out demons (see Matt. 10:1; Luke 10:17; Acts 8:7). It is the most common variety to be found throughout the New Testament.

2. *Occult-level spiritual warfare,* which deals with demonic powers at work in occultic practices that appear to go considerably beyond the simple possession of an individual by a demon. Paul's Philippi encounter with a demon-possessed fortune-teller who annoyed the apostle for many days was cited as an example (see Acts 16:16-24).

3. *Strategic-level spiritual warfare,* that appears to reach an even higher level of conflict. The intercessor now contends against a much greater concentration of demonic powers, those which are increasingly being defined as territorial spirits.

The subject of territoriality of high-level demonic entities (that is, territorial spirits thought to be assigned to specific geographic regions) is one of considerable debate among certain biblical scholars. But the apostle Paul made it clear that something satanic and unmistakably real is indeed "out there." Whether we like to talk about it or not, they're organized! Paul refers to these entities as "rulers," "authorities," "powers of this dark world" and "spiritual forces of evil in the heavenly realms" (Eph. 6:12, NIV).

According to Wagner:

> A clear biblical account of strategic-level spiritual warfare is obviously found in Revelation 12 where we are told, "War broke out in heaven: Michael and his angels fought against the dragon; and the dragon and his angels fought" (Rev. 12:7).[3]

Understanding Strongholds

At the heart of almost all discussion of strategic-level warfare is the subject of enemy strongholds and how our prayers seek to weaken and remove these spiritual fortresses. The New Testament term *stronghold* comes from the Greek word *ochuroma* which means simply "to fortify through holding" or "a place of protection, such as a castle."

A basic look at the makeup of this word in English provides a most succinct and helpful definition. *Strong* simply means "power." A person who is strong has power, whether referring to brute strength or authority. To *hold*, of course, is to "grip." Thus, a *stronghold* is a "power grip." Inherent in the Greek definition "to fortify through holding" is the suggestion that as this "power grip" continues, it grows increasingly stronger because that which is being held is growing constantly weaker. It is like a mighty python squeezing all the strength out of its victim. The python appears to be getting stronger because its victim is actually getting weaker.

A stronghold, then, can be any fortified place Satan establishes to position and exalt himself against the knowledge and purposes of God. Further, it is any fortified dwelling used as a means of protection from an attacker or enemy committed to penetrating and looting another's camp.

A stronghold can also be any fortified set of thought patterns and ideas that govern individuals, communities, nations, churches, religions or other controlling institutions of influence.

Note again the Greek word *ochuroma* that suggests "to fortify." When something is fortified, it is made stronger by its ingredients or components. For example, we look for cereal on the grocery shelf that is fortified with certain vitamins. When highways are made, the concrete is often fortified (made stronger) with steel.

Thus, a stronghold of the enemy is that which has been fortified through a variety of ideas and thought patterns, often reaffirmed over many generations, that tend to make that stronghold increasingly difficult to penetrate.

The Argentine missions strategist Edgardo Silvoso, of Harvest Evangelism, offers this added definition:

> A stronghold is a mind-set impregnated with hopelessness that causes us to accept as unchangeable something that we know is contrary to the will of God.[4]

Silvoso uses the example of a comprehensive strategy that was developed to evangelize the city of Resistencia in Argentina. When first visiting the city, Silvoso quickly discovered there were two very distinct strongholds, or mind-sets, seriously affecting the thinking of the church: *disunity* and *apathy toward the lost.* So strong was the disunity, for example, that many leaders had reached the conclusion it was simply unchangeable even though they knew this to be clearly contrary to the will of God.

Concerning apathy toward the lost, Edgardo was equally amazed to discover a mind-set permeating the thinking of many believers. No matter what evangelism activities the churches might engage in corporately, when all their efforts were concluded there would still be far more lost people than those saved. And this was in spite of the apostle Peter's definitive statement that God is "not willing that any should perish but that all should come to repentance" (2 Pet. 3:9).

The fact was that, after much intensive effort, the church in Resistencia grew by almost 30 percent in the months following the intensive prayer-and-evangelism strategy.

The enemy of the church has, indeed, attempted to gain a

foothold within the church and globally seeks to exalt himself in every possible way to maintain his generations-long "holdings."

Consider Paul's reference to "every high thing that exalts itself against...God" (2 Cor. 10:5) in his analysis of the believers' weaponry. The expression *high thing* comes from the Greek word *hypsoma* and includes several important definitions. According to the *Dictionary of New Testament Theology,* one definition of *hypsoma* is "powers directed against God, seeking to intervene between God and man." *High,* of course, refers to position. *Thing* speaks of an entity or concept. *High thing* thus refers to a spiritual concept or entity that has an elevated position from which it intends to exalt itself against God and His purposes.

Note especially the definition "powers directed against God, seeking to intervene between God and man." This may well refer to demonically controlled or manipulated "satanic" intercessors. As shocking as it may seem, there is growing evidence that a ministry of satanic intercession is being carried out by committed Satan worshippers globally.

I recall hearing the testimony of a Christian lady who, while flying on a commercial airliner, noticed that the woman next to her had politely declined her meal. She explained to the flight attendant that she was fasting that day. The Christian lady, assuming she was sitting beside a fellow believer, joyously said, "How nice to be sitting beside another Christian." To that her neighbor replied tersely, "Oh, I'm not a Christian. I'm a Satan worshipper, and I'm fasting today for the break-up of marriages among Christian leaders."

Could demonically inspired intercessors actually be having an impact on such things as the marriages of Christian leaders? Perhaps it is not without significance that as similar reports of satanic intercession increase, a corresponding number of prominent church leaders globally are seeing their marriages and ministries come under severe attack through immorality and lust. Could it be the enemy is more organized in this regard than we think? If so, what are concerned believers to do?

Extraordinary Prayer

Perhaps the answer is to be found in a fresh commitment to what might be defined as extraordinary, strategic-level prayer.

Ordinary praying (though no prayer that touches God is ever truly ordinary) would appear to be insufficient for the battles that dot the spiritual landscape of a church truly committed to fulfill the Great Commission in this generation.

The idea of a level of prayer that moves beyond the ordinary is really nothing new. In 1746, Jonathan Edwards reportedly issued a powerful call for "concerted prayer" that he referred to as "extraordinary prayer." A widely circulated pamphlet by the Puritan evangelist was instrumental in issuing this call. Its title was rather lengthy: *An Humble Attempt to Promote Explicit Agreement and Visible Union of God's People in Extraordinary Prayer for the Revival of the Church and the Advancement of Christ's Kingdom on Earth*.

The title itself was much of the message. God was calling His people to higher levels of prayer that went well beyond mere personal material concerns. The focus was a passionate, corporate seeking of God for a massive spiritual awakening that would sweep through the church, resulting in the spreading of the gospel of Jesus Christ to the ends of the earth. The record shows this call was heeded, resulting in what historians describe as the Great Awakening and the saving of America's early colonies from almost certain collapse.

Today a similar call is ringing throughout the church for the pursuit of new levels of extraordinary prayer, including prayer that is strategic in its focus. Of course, none of this is to suggest that faithful, devotional prayer is ever to be judged as ordinary or insignificant. Most believers would no doubt evaluate much of their personal times of prayer as rather ordinary. The fact is, faithfulness in daily devotional prayer may well prove to be the key in preparing believers for the intensity of the warfare that most certainly awaits the church in its final assault on Satan's earthly domain.

Still, in all of our faithful devotional preparation, it would do well for us to give at least some thought to the basics of strategic-level praying so we'll not be uninitiated when the call comes from our Captain enlisting us in the frontline battle for the nations. Our next chapter should help you understand these "basics." ⊠

EIGHT

STRATEGIC-LEVEL PRAYER

*Seven Qualities for
Aggressive Warfare Intercession*

PRAYER IS the final armament!" wrote Wesley Duewel. "Prayer is the all-inclusive strategy of war. It is a form of spiritual bombing to saturate any area before God's army of witnesses begin their advance. Prayer is the all-conquering, invincible weapon of the army of God."[1]

Duewel's description of prayer in battle terms is appropriate preparation for a more careful look at strategic-level prayer. Although there is no doubt a multitude of ways to define such praying, seven specific qualities come to mind.

1. Strategic-Level Praying Is *Authoritative.*

Authoritative praying is perhaps best described in God's powerful promise to Jeremiah: "See, I have this day set you over the nations and over the kingdoms, to root out and to pull down, to destroy and to throw down, to build and to plant" (Jer. 1:10). Authoritative praying is to recognize that our very words, spoken with the authority invested in the promises of God, enable us to confront enemy strongholds by rooting out, pulling down, destroying and throwing down, as well as building and planting.

A remarkable testimony from the life of Reformation leader Martin Luther uniquely illustrates authoritative prayer. In 1540 Luther's close friend Frederick Myconius was taken seriously ill and lay on his deathbed. Myconius had been one of Luther's dearest friends and supporters during the difficult days of the Reformation. Barely able to speak and given but a few days to live by his doctor, Myconius wrote with trembling hand what he thought would be his final letter to Luther.

When Luther received the letter, he was so disturbed at the thought of losing his dear friend that he sat down and immediately wrote a most unusual response. He seemed convinced that God would keep Myconius alive at least long enough to receive his reply.

"I command thee in the name of God to live," Luther wrote, "because I still have need of thee in the work of reforming the church. The Lord will never let me hear that thou art dead but will permit thee to survive me."

The brief but powerful letter ended with this incredible statement: "For this I am praying, this is my will, and may my will be done, because I seek only to glorify the name of God."[2]

The record shows that Frederick Myconius did indeed remain alive long enough to receive Luther's letter. Further, as the communiqué was read, God's presence filled the room where he lay. Within days the health of Myconius was completely restored. The record further shows that he did not die until two months after Luther's death six years later in 1546. Authoritative prayer, at a level of obvious strategic significance, had robbed Satan of an almost-certain victory.

2. Strategic-Level Praying Is *Combative.*

Combat is an absolute of war. Imagine a war without combat. And because our warfare for the nations is as real as any battle ever to be waged, we must recognize the combative nature of the conflict.

Paul employed battle language when he appealed to Roman believers.

> Now I beg you, brethren, through the Lord Jesus Christ, and through the love of the Spirit, that you strive together with me in prayers to God for me (Rom. 15:30).

The expression "strive together with me" pictures someone who is engaged in direct combat and is appealing for assistance. Here Paul is suggesting that his success in battle depends upon the prayers of others who are not physically with him but who pray for him.

Consider also Paul's admonition to Ephesian believers to "put on the whole armor of God, that you may be able to stand against the wiles of the devil" (Eph. 6:11). The expression "stand against" is from the same Greek expression translated "resist" in James 4:7 where we're instructed to "resist the devil" in order that he might "flee from you." Regarding this combative nature of prayer, the gifted Boston preacher S. D. Gordon said almost a century ago:

> To define prayer, one must use the language of war. Peace language is not equal to the situation. The earth is in a state of war and is being hotly besieged. Thus, one must use war talk to grasp the facts with which prayer is concerned.[3]

Although some may be uncomfortable in referring to prayer in militant battle terms, the Scriptures are filled with battle analogies in describing the believer's warfare. In fact, the very phrase *Lord of hosts* is itself a battle term describing our Lord. It appears some 273 times in the Old Testament. (The old English word *host* actually means "army.")

When Joshua encountered Christ at Jericho as described earlier, he met Him as Commander of the army of the Lord, or, in today's terminology, the "Commander-in-chief" of the heavenly army (Josh. 5:14-15).

New Testament analogies of the believer's battle also abound. We're told to "fight the good fight of faith" (1 Tim. 6:12) and to "endure hardship...like a good soldier of Christ Jesus" (2 Tim. 2:3, NIV). Paul further expands on this theme, declaring:

> No one serving as a soldier gets involved in civilian affairs — he wants to please his commanding officer (2 Tim. 2:4, NIV).

To Roman believers the apostle admonishes, "Put on the armor of light" (Rom. 13:12, NIV). To Ephesian saints it is "the full armor of God" (Eph. 6:11, NIV). Corinthian believers also were told:

> The weapons we fight with are not the weapons of the world (2 Cor. 10:4, NIV).

Strategic-level prayer merely recognizes and acknowledges this combat reality of Scripture and takes it boldly into our praying. It is not necessarily loud or noisy prayer, but it *is* prayer bathed with scriptural aggression and saturated with a bold militancy.

3. Strategic-Level Praying Is *Intensive.*

James seems to have understood the difference between ordinary prayer and passionate, fervent prayer.

> The effective, fervent prayer of a righteous man avails much (James 5:16).

The essence of the Greek text of this passage suggests a praying that is divinely energized by the presence of the Holy Spirit causing the person praying to manifest a fervent intensity that becomes effective in its workings. To be intense is to be absorbed in a task or focus. It implies total concentration in a matter. When applied to prayer, intensity is to become so convinced that our fervency in prayer makes a difference that not to pray with passion would assure us of a total absence of results.

When the apostle James refers to this kind of praying, he pictures a level of warfare prayer that is beyond the believer's normal spiritual capacity. It is prayer divinely energized by the direct involvement of the Holy Spirit. Although the word *fervent* actually does not appear in the Greek text of James 5:16, it is an appropriate amplification or extension of the word *effectual* which does appear in the Greek text. All of this flows from the Greek word *energeo,* a word meaning "effectual" or "that which is effective." Yet simply to say prayer is effective when offered by a righteous person was deemed by the translators to be shallow to the context. Therefore, *fervent* was rightly added to the text. The fact that the following verses use Elijah's passionate, earnest prayers for rain as an example strengthens this interpretation.

Energeo actually is derived from the Greek expression *energes* which, in Hebrews 4:12, is translated "powerful."

> For the word of God is living and *powerful,* and sharper
> than any two-edged sword (italics added).

In 1 Corinthians 16:9, *energes* is translated "effective" in describing an open door for the gospel that allowed its message to become effective wherever it was preached. Applied to the James text, all this suggests that our praying, when energized by the power of the Holy Spirit, makes things happen. Our prayers work!

Such fervency, or intensity in prayer, is frequently found in Scripture. Isaiah, for example, demonstrated this kind of intensity when he cried out for God to rend the heavens so that God's glory might melt the mountains (see Is. 64:1-7). Especially note the intensity in Isaiah's use of the word *rend,* which literally means "tear open." The prophet seems to be pleading for a violent response from God to his petition.

Interestingly, a New Testament type of prayer that fits this Old Testament category of intensive prayer is the New Testament word *supplication.* From the Greek word *deesis,* supplication means a strong incessant pleading that persists until the answer comes (see Eph. 6:18).

Closely related to this divinely inspired intensity in prayer is the recurring biblical theme of "travail" (see Is. 53:11; 66:7-9). Travail is a picture of desperate prayer, not unlike that of the prayer of Ezra when the scribe discovered that many leaders in Israel, including the priests and Levites, had not separated themselves from the abominations of the people with whom they dwelt (see Ezra 9:3-6). Ezra's intensity was such that he pulled out some of his hair along with portions of his beard. He then fell on his face with his hands stretched to God in total humility.

Christ Himself is Scripture's best example of this kind of intensity in travail. In Gethsemane, Jesus prayed "more earnestly," and "His sweat became like great drops of blood falling down to the ground" (Luke 22:44). The author of the letter to the Hebrews would later describe Christ as offering up "prayers and supplications, with vehement cries and tears" (Heb. 5:7). This is certainly not ordinary prayer.

Intensive prayer no doubt pleases God because "crying out" to Him with such fervency indicates the warrior has finally reached the point of true desperation. He or she has nowhere else to turn but to the Lord. At the heart of such praying is a spirit of determination saturated with a Holy Spirit-empowered fervency that refuses to give up until the answer comes. It is warfare prayer that wins!

4. Strategic-Level Praying Is *Confrontive.*

Prayer at a strategic level, because of its very nature, will be confrontive. Peter dealt directly with the infirmity of a crippled man at the Gate Beautiful (Acts 3:1-4). Jesus admonished His disciples to command mountains to move (Mark 11:23). In the same way, our confrontation will often be directly with the obstacle.

Spiritual mountains or obstacles that stand in the way of either God's "fullness" upon the church or the resulting "fulfillment" of the Great Commission obviously need to be removed. And to pray specifically (note Jesus said, "*this* mountain" — Mark 11:23), we need to identify the obstacles. This is why intercessors engaging in warfare at a strategic level must do their homework in preparing for prayer and learn to listen carefully to the voice of the Holy Spirit while they are praying.

Especially note Christ's dialogue with His disciples regarding their promised authority to command mountains to move. The experience occurs the day following Christ's triumphal entry into Jerusalem as He and His disciples depart for Bethany. There Jesus observes a fig tree with enough leaves to indicate it should possess

93

ripe figs, even though it was not the normal season for fig trees to be producing (see Mark 11:12-14). Nonetheless, nearing the tree, Jesus notices it has no figs and promptly curses it, declaring, "Let no one eat fruit from you ever again" (Mark 11:14). The disciples had little idea this authoritative act was to become the heart of a lesson Jesus would soon teach them on how to take direct action against spiritual obstacles erected by the enemy.

The following morning the complete lesson was presented (see Mark 11:20-24). As the disciples, led by Jesus, again passed the fig tree, they noticed it had withered completely from its very roots (v. 20). Peter quickly reminded Jesus this was the tree He had cursed only a day earlier. In response to Peter's observation, Jesus issued a far-reaching command:

> Have faith in God. For assuredly, I say to you, whoever says to this mountain, "Be removed and be cast into the sea," and does not doubt in his heart, but believes that those things he says will be done, he will have whatever he says (Mark 11:22-23).

Christ was saying there would be certain situations where the disciples would find it necessary to take direct authority in spiritual matters, provided they did so with unwavering faith.

On a later occasion, just prior to His final Gethsemane "warfare" experience, Jesus would say to His disciples, "And whatever you ask in My name, that I will do" (John 14:13). He was implying that He would intervene directly on their behalf if they learned to employ the authority of His name in prayer. It is on this occasion that Jesus extends to His disciples what might be defined as a supernatural "power of attorney."

The full meaning of the Greek word *atteo*, translated in John 14:13 simply as "ask," is essential to our understanding of strategic-level prayer. *Atteo* also means to "claim," "demand" or "require." Perhaps the best way to grasp what Jesus meant in saying "whatever you ask in My name, that I will do" is to observe how His disciples interpreted this promise since they heard Him speak it in their native tongue.

The answer is to be found in the early chapters of Acts (see Acts 3:1-7) where we discover the first recorded instance of any of the disciples exercising this unique power of attorney. Peter and John had come to the Gate Beautiful and met a crippled man who, at more than forty years of age, had never taken a single step. His sole provision from day to day depended on begging. He thus pleads with Peter and John for a contribution. Peter, however, promptly employs the name of Jesus, commanding the man in Jesus' name to rise up and walk. Interestingly, Peter also gives the man a lift up to his feet as if to urge him on in his faith (v. 7).

Of special significance in this lesson is that Peter actually does not ask God to do *anything* in this circumstance. He simply recognizes this occasion as one that fits the conditions he believed Jesus implied when He said, "You shall make a claim based on my name, and it shall be done!" In the case of this infirm man, his infirmity was the "mountain" (Mark 11:23) that had to be confronted directly.

Jesus did not say to His disciples, "Ask God to remove the mountain." Instead He said, "You command the mountain to move." He further instructed them to make claims based on His name. Therefore Peter felt he had clear authority to do so. His action proved to be correct by the miracle that followed — a miracle that resulted not only in a lame man walking but in at least five thousand souls coming to a knowledge of Jesus as the Messiah (Acts 4:4).

We see something of this same confrontive quality of our warfare in Matthew's description of Christ's advancing kingdom. He writes:

> From the days of John the Baptist until now, the kingdom of heaven has been forcefully advancing, and forceful men lay hold of it (Matt. 11:12, NIV).

The New King James Version reads:

> The kingdom of heaven suffers violence, and the violent take it by force.

Explaining this text, Jack Hayford writes:

> Jesus here asserts the "violence" of the kingdom. The unique grammatical construction of the text does not make clear if the kingdom of God is the victim of vio-

lence or if, as the kingdom advances in victory, it does so through violent, spiritual conflict and warfare. But the context does. Jesus' immediate references to the nonreligious style of John and the confrontive, miraculous ministry of Elijah teach that the kingdom of God makes its penetration by a kind of violent entry opposing the human status quo.[4]

To engage in confrontive prayer at a strategic level, then, is to oppose the status quo of demonic dominion over a region and to do so with a confident, Holy Spirit-inspired tenacity.

5. Strategic-Level Praying Is *Comprehensive.*

Jesus spoke of the comprehensive nature of believing prayer when He said, "And whatever things you ask in prayer, believing, you will receive" (Matt. 21:22). "Whatever" is certainly comprehensive. We can have "whatever" we ask! But how sensitive are we to the "whatevers" of our praying? How focused are they? How full of God's purposes and priorities are our prayers? Like those highly trained special forces units in the military, we need to be trained in how to make our prayers truly comprehensive and thus much more effective.

Industrialist Henry Ford learned a unique lesson about approaching difficult problems comprehensively. The huge generators supplying electricity to his automotive assembly plant had suddenly shut down. None of his engineers could isolate the problem. Ford immediately contacted his old friend Charles Steinmetz, the gifted electrical engineer. With but a few tools, Steinmetz began tinkering around several of the large generators. In a matter of a few hours, the genius had located and corrected the problem by poking a screwdriver into just the right spot.

Several days later the industrialist received a bill from his friend requesting the then incredible sum of $10,000. Being close friends, Ford immediately wrote Steinmetz, questioning why he would charge so exorbitant an amount just for a few minutes of tinkering. Steinmetz promptly responded with a letter adjusting the bill, with an added written explanation. The bill now read: "$10.00 for tinkering," to which was added, "$9,990.00 for knowing where to tinker."

Effective strategic-level intercessors must know "where to tinker" with their prayers if they are to learn the secret of praying comprehensively. Certainly, a key to such prayer is to understand the necessity of Holy Spirit-anointed "revelation insight" to guide us in our praying.

The experience of the prophet Jeremiah provides a special understanding of this important subject. Few Bible verses are quoted more frequently on the subject of prayer's power than Jeremiah 33:3. God tells Jeremiah:

> Call to Me, and I will answer you, and show you great and mighty things, which you do not know.

God is actually speaking to the imprisoned prophet Jeremiah a second time, confirming His earlier warning that Jerusalem would be destroyed by the Chaldeans (see Jer. 32:26-28). God further confirms that Israel will ultimately be restored to her own land and shall be blessed someday with the coming Messiah. In this context God promises Jeremiah that if He will call to Him, He not only will answer him, but He will reveal to him "great and *mighty* things" which could not otherwise be known. The word *mighty* (from the Hebrew *batsar*) is better rendered "isolated" or "inaccessible." The suggestion is that God would reveal to Jeremiah, by "revelation insight," things that otherwise would be inaccessible or isolated from his understanding.

Such "revelation insight" always has been essential for a clear understanding of victorious warfare. It is certainly vital to those who would seek to pray comprehensively. Surely, one cannot pray comprehensively without God-given insight into how to pray intelligently and strategically. According to God's promise to Jeremiah, what might appear in the natural to be isolated or inaccessible will be revealed as we call upon Him.

The apostle Paul, too, recognized the need to pray for such comprehensive insight. In his letter to Ephesian believers he spoke of his faithful prayers on their behalf, reminding them:

> I keep asking that the God of our Lord Jesus Christ, the glorious Father, may give you the Spirit of wisdom and revelation, so that you may know him better. I pray also

that the eyes of your heart may be enlightened in order
that you may know the hope to which he has called you
(Eph. 1:17-18, NIV).

To be enlightened, of course, is to have light shed on an otherwise isolated or inaccessible fact. It is to receive revelation insight that, in the case of strategic-level prayer, helps us to pray more comprehensively.

6. Strategic-Level Praying Is *Creative.*

We return again to God's powerful call in the young life of the prophet Jeremiah:

See, I have this day set you over the nations and over the
kingdoms...to build and to plant (Jer. 1:10).

Pulling down, rooting out and even destroying a stronghold (all a part of Jeremiah's mandate) were not the concluding focuses to his prophetic calling. Jeremiah was also to build and to plant. He was to "pray into place" creatively that which God wanted to raise up in the place of those strongholds that were removed.

There's a unique parallel to this Jeremiah lesson for us to consider today in the once communist-controlled Central Asian republics of the current Commonwealth of Independent States (the old Soviet Union). Christians of the region, though few in number, are ready to plant the gospel, house to house, before Islam raises itself up to become an even stronger obstacle than was communism.

Creative prayer would be to pray into existence the release of financial resources for the printing of evangelistic literature for such ministries as Every Home for Christ, the massive release of tools such as the *JESUS* film from Campus Crusade for Christ and the saturation planting of churches throughout these regions before it's too late. We've rooted out and prayed down a stronghold (communism), but now an even greater stronghold (Islam) could well take its place unless we plant and build the church of Jesus Christ quickly in these areas.

What is it to pray creatively? Creative prayer is prayer that allows us to become a part of God's creative process in bringing His purposes to pass. When Paul wrote to believers at Rome, he reminded them of the miracle that took place in Abraham's life. God had promised to make Abraham a father of many nations, even though the likelihood of this occurring appeared impossible. But, as Paul explained, Abraham believed in a "God, who gives life to the dead and calls those things which do not exist as though they did" (Rom. 4:17). This is the secret to creative prayer. It is tapping into an Abraham-like faith that enables us to speak prayerfully into existence that which we are convinced is the will of God.

Faith, of course, is essential to creative prayer. The author of Hebrews defines such faith, and the Amplified New Testament expands the definition.

> Now faith is the assurance (the confirmation, the title-deed) of the things [we] hope for, being the proof of things [we] do not see and the conviction of their reality — faith perceiving as real fact what is not revealed to the senses (Heb. 11:1, AMP).

Commenting on this definition, an anonymous believer once said, "Faith is reaching into nowhere, grabbing hold of nothing and holding on until it becomes something."

Creative prayer, then, is to understand that our words, transformed into prayer, can release something of God's presence into a situation that might otherwise never experience His touch. Creative prayer is prayer that sees into the invisible, captures something of the heart and plan of God for that which is seen, and then fervently and boldly speaks it into existence.

7. Strategic-Level Praying Is *Decisive.*

The final quality of strategic-level prayer is, in a sense, the sum of the other six. Strategic-level prayer is decisive. *Webster's* dictionary defines decisive as "resolute, determined, unmistakable and unquestionable." It represents something conclusive. It also means "having the power or quality of deciding."[5]

Veteran intercessors realize that their authority enables them to participate directly in the outcome of the final battle of history to *dethrone* Satan and *enthrone* Christ over the nations. This is why

99

the decisive victory of Revelation 12:7-12, where Satan is banished forever from the heavenlies by Michael the archangel and his army of heavenly angels, is of such interest to intercessors. As suggested earlier, none of this will transpire until first an angel with a golden censer (Rev. 8:3) pours out the prayers of all the saints upon the altar of heaven. Only then will Christ's kingdom be fully established "forever and ever" (Rev. 11:15). But this all begins with that "decisive" release of the prayers of the saints. Intercessors who become weary in their warfare would do well to remember that our victory is already assured. We only must fight.

Note Paul's concluding promise to Roman believers that "the God of peace will crush Satan under your feet shortly" (Rom. 16:20). The word *crush* is from the Greek *suntribo* meaning "to trample upon, break in pieces, shatter, bruise, grind down, and smash." What could be more decisive? Indeed, our victory is decisive in every way. It is assured over the world (1 John 5:4-5), over the flesh (Gal. 5:24; Rom. 7:22-25), over all that exalts itself against God (2 Cor. 10:5) and even over death and the grave (1 Cor. 15:54-55).

Paul spoke of this decisiveness in both of his Corinthian letters. First, he wrote:

> But thanks be to God, who gives us the victory through our Lord Jesus Christ (1 Cor. 15:57).

Second, he declared:

> But thanks be to God, who always leads us in triumphant procession in Christ and through us spreads everywhere the fragrance of the knowledge of him (2 Cor. 2:14, NIV).

From ancient times victory over the enemies of God's purposes has been assured. God told Israel:

> You will pursue your enemies, and they will fall by the sword before you. Five of you will chase a hundred, and a hundred of you will chase ten thousand, and your enemies will fall by the sword before you (Lev. 26:7-8, NIV).

Elsewhere we read:

> When you go to war against your enemies and see horses and chariots and an army greater than yours, do not be afraid of them, because the Lord your God, who brought you up out of Egypt, will be with you (Deut. 20:1, NIV).

Later Moses declared:

> For the Lord your God is the one who goes with you to fight for you against your enemies to give you victory (Deut. 20:4, NIV).

What God has begun in and through His people will be accomplished. He only looks for a generation of courageous believers truly committed to fulfilling the commission He has given His church through His Son. What Christ has initiated at the cross He will finish with closure! Jesus is, after all, "the author and finisher of our faith" (Heb. 12:2). ⧗

NINE

CONTENDING FOR THE LOST

*Establishing Siege Strategies for
Our Loved Ones, Cities and Nations*

WILLIAM CAREY is often referred to as the father of modern missions. A brilliant youth with a promising future, Carey was moved by God in his early years with a passion for the lost that changed the course of mission's history.

Working as a shoe cobbler's assistant in eighteenth century England, young Carey is said to have saved discarded scraps of shoe leather from which he fashioned a makeshift globe. Hours spent in a local library with the best maps of the then known world gave Carey enough insight to sketch in ink the outlines of the continents and countries on his crude leather globe.

Decades later, it was said that Carey's tears of intercession during those early years literally blurred the outlines of the nations on his handmade globe. They ultimately gave rise to his calling to become a pioneer missionary to distant India.

Did Carey's tears make a difference? Some might question the missionary's evangelism effectiveness — seven years transpired before he saw his first convert. But I believe his greatest contribution to the evangelization of India was those tearful prayers poured over the nations of the world, including his primary love — India. In fact, I firmly believe Carey's prayers for India are still being answered.

Every Home for Christ, the ministry I have the joy of directing, systematically takes a printed salvation message, each with a decision card, to every home in a nation. In recent years we launched our final phase of taking the gospel — for the third time — to all 600,000 villages in India. (EHC has had similar campaigns in 147 nations.) The first full coverage of India required ten years of intensive commitment involving as many as ten thousand volunteer distributors at any given time along with hundreds of full-time workers.

But the harvest was amazing. In the first coverage more than one million people responded to our invitation to accept Christ or enroll in a Bible correspondence course by sending in decision cards to our nine regional Indian offices during a ten-year period. Since then, an additional 3.9 million response cards have been received from subsequent coverages, and as many as seventeen new village churches are being planted daily. Truly, Carey's tears for India that began with his crude globe may be reaping a harvest far beyond anything the pioneer missionary had ever imagined.

Laying Siege in Prayer

Praying over a map or a globe, as was the case with William Carey, is not new in biblical terms. Centuries ago, God commissioned Ezekiel to lay siege to the geographic region of Jerusalem using a man-made map. God told the prophet:

> Now, son of man, take a clay tablet, put it in front of you and draw the city of Jerusalem on it. Then lay siege to it (Ezek. 4:1-2, NIV).

103

What does it mean to "lay siege" in prayer? *Siege* means "the act or process of surrounding and attacking a fortified place in such a way as to isolate it from help and supplies for the purpose of lessening the resistance of the defenders and thereby making capture possible." Another definition reads: "any prolonged or persistent effort to overcome resistance." A third, more ancient definition reads: "a seat of rule." (See the *Random House Dictionary of English Language*.) Taken together, laying siege in prayer would suggest a strategy that involves the spiritual surrounding and blockading of an enemy fortress; it could potentially involve a prolonged commitment that leads to a transfer of the seat of authority in either a specific situation or geographic area.

When God spoke to Ezekiel to "lay siege" to a hand-drawn map of Jerusalem, he used the Hebrew word *matsuwr* which means "something hemming in," "a mound" or "a stronghold or tower." *Matsuwr* comes from the prime Hebrew root *tsuwr* which means "to cramp, confine, assault, bind up or enclose."

In Ezekiel's day, drawing the outline of Jerusalem on a clay tablet would be today's equivalent of a person sketching a map on a piece of paper. Of course, printed maps are very common today. If Ezekiel's experience had taken place in our generation, the Lord probably would have told him simply to find a map of Jerusalem and lay siege to it through prayer. One thing is clear — Ezekiel was to involve himself in a symbolic state of warfare regarding Jerusalem. Similarly, we can lay siege to local or global strongholds using a map of our city, nation or world. The same might apply to laying siege in prayer for a loved one by taking a picture of that person and using it as a focus for intensive prayer.

Laying Siege: the Ezekiel Model

After the Lord commanded Ezekiel to draw a map of the city of Jerusalem on a clay tablet, He added:

> Lay siege against it, build a siege wall against it, and heap up a mound against it; set camps against it also, and place battering rams against it all around. Moreover take for yourself an iron plate, and set it as an iron wall between you and the city. Set your face against it, and it

shall be besieged, and you shall lay siege against it (Ezek. 4:2-3).

A careful examination of the five specific directives the Lord gave Ezekiel should prove helpful to our developing a practical plan to lay siege to the lost — whether close friends, loved ones or even unreached people groups in distant nations whose names we may not know. These directives include:

1. Build a Siege Wall Against It!

The Hebrew word for "siege wall" is *dayeg* which is translated in the King James Version of Scripture as "fort." It refers to a watchtower. Various translations employ different terms for *dayeg*. The NIV translates it "siege works," whereas the NAS uses "siege wall," as does the New King James Version. The New English Bible translates it "watch-towers." Interestingly, a direct literal translation of the Hebrew word would perhaps best render *dayeg* as simply a "battering tower."

We do know that setting a battering tower or watchtower in place would serve the initial purpose of observing the situation under siege. Thus, to build a "fort" or a "watchtower" against a potential enemy fortress means to establish a launching pad for the initial assault needed to begin the siege. Key to that observation tower would be some plan or means to gather intelligence. No army would attack an enemy without some knowledge or understanding of the enemy's capabilities.

The same is true of our strategic praying. We must understand the schemes of our enemy which is no doubt why Jesus spoke of our need both to "watch and pray" (Matt. 26:41).

Thankfully, intercessors of late appear to be recognizing the need for much more accurate "targeting" information of our enemy's intentions to help them in their strategic praying. As George Otis Jr., author of two challenging books, *The Last of the Giants* and *The Twilight Labyrinth,* reminds us, accurate targeting coordinates are critical if our prayers are to be focused in such a way as to do the most damage to Satan's fortresses.

Saddam Hussein's launching of Scud missiles during the Persian Gulf War versus America's launching of "smart bombs" and "Patriot missiles" is an interesting analogy. When Hussein launched a Scud missile, as Otis reminds us, the Iraqi dictator had to turn on CNN to see where it landed. America's smart bombs, however, would go into a very specific window or down the chimney of a particular building at the exact pretargeted address. The difference was a technologically advanced system employing specific targeting coordinates that were obtained as the result of highly sophisticated intelligence gathering.

Especially important to note in our Ezekiel warfare model is that the prophet is told to build a "siege wall" or "fort" against *it*. The *it* in the text is *not* the city but the clay tablet or map of the city. Ezekiel was not told to confront the actual city physically at any time. He was simply instructed to focus his spiritual energies on his hand-drawn map, trusting that his obedience in the spiritual realm would ultimately release something of God's power into the physical realm.

2. Cast Up a Mount Against It!

A mount in ancient times was a rise or elevated path that might serve as a means to reach the top of a high wall that typically surrounded cities in Ezekiel's day. A mount was thus an incline up a wall. The New English Bible translates this expression "siege-ramp." It suggests the establishing of a means to penetrate a city. It was to involve some sort of preparation to initiate such an assault.

We see a similar call to preparation in Isaiah's prophetic command, "Go through, go through the gates! Prepare the way for the people; build up, build up the highway! Take out the stones, lift up a banner for the peoples!" (Is. 62:10).

Note the symbolism in Isaiah's lesson to would-be siege warriors of today. Before we can seize new territory for Jesus by evangelizing the lost of a region, certain aspects of spiritual preparation must be made regarding these areas. Prayer-saturated strategic planning will be included, making possible the ultimate assault and penetration into the region.

In practical terms, to "cast up a mount" in establishing siege strategies for a region is to pray that God will provide the right instruction and preparation for those who might go into that area with the gospel.

3. Set Up a Camp Against It!

Ezekiel is next told to establish a camp against his map of the city. Again we note that he is not directed to set a camp against the city but against the *map* of the city.

Camp comes from the Hebrew word *machaneh* which means "an encampment of travelers" or "a collection of tents for warriors who are preparing for battle."

The New English Bible uniquely translates this passage, "Put mantelets in position." *Mantelet* is a somewhat archaic term used to describe a movable shelter employed as a means of protection when attacking an enemy. Perhaps the nearest equivalent in today's context would be "a bulletproof shelter or screen" (see the *Random House Dictionary of English Language*). Riot police of today, when confronting huge crowds of angry demonstrators, often hold large bulletproof shields (or "mantelets") to protect themselves against attack. Mantelets, of course, are movable.

Ezekiel's siege model would thus suggest that there are some aspects of the army that are not positioned permanently but that move about. For proper positioning of an army as it establishes its siege strategy, some troops no doubt must be organized into smaller groups (perhaps like those special forces mentioned earlier) who are able to spread out to various areas at a moment's notice. Whereas there's a main fortress from which principal activity is directed, there must be the "mantelets" or camps set up ready to move at any time into the battle.

The emerging Jericho Center at Colorado Springs with its growing number of related Jericho chapters would be at least one modern spiritual example of this aspect of the Ezekiel model. The Jericho Center with its strategic praying and networking of ministries for the task of breaking through barriers into unevangelized regions of the world would be more like the fort or watchtower using the Ezekiel picture. The Jericho chapters, those small prayer teams of special forces positioned throughout the world, would be like the camps or mantelets.

The main center is more of a central location from which to observe enemy activity and carry out meaningful strategies to penetrate those regions controlled by the enemy. But the smaller, more mobile camps are scattered everywhere for the purpose of both gathering meaningful intelligence for the continuing conflict and actually engaging in that conflict when called upon to do so by the Holy Spirit.

Key to our praying regarding the application of this aspect of the Ezekiel siege model is to ask God to raise up thousands of these mantelets or small strategic prayer camps (Jericho chapters) for the serious warfare that lies ahead. (For specific information on being a part of Every Home for Christ's growing army of Jericho chapters, write: Every Home for Christ, P. O. Box 35950, Colorado Springs, CO 80935-3595.)

4. *Set Battering Rams Against It!*

Ezekiel's siege model continues with instructions to set "battering rams" against his hand-drawn map. A battering ram in Ezekiel's day was a huge beam of wood suspended on chains within a movable tower. Using a battering ram in an assault thus would suggest a repetitive hammering away at an obstacle or wall that stands in the way of laying siege to a fortress.

Again, we are reminded that the word *siege* not only implies a carefully planned strategy for penetrating a fortress, but it suggests a potentially prolonged duration before the fortress is captured. Using a battering ram accurately pictures part of the duration process; rarely does a wall fall with one blow — except, of course, if God initiates the blow as was true at Jericho. But even in the case of Jericho, a certain degree of duration was involved spiritually in the seven days of marching. Some walls clearly will fall only as the result of a spiritual hammering away. We recall that Paul admonished Thessalonian believers to "pray without ceasing" (1 Thess. 5:17).

Also significant to the Ezekiel model is how the prophet is told to set battering rams against the map of the city "all around" (NEB). This suggests confronting a stronghold or fortress from every angle so as to assure complete victory. It speaks of a thoroughness in our warfare that doesn't allow pockets of spiritual guerrilla forces to remain in a region hindering the ongoing purposes of God in the area.

But perhaps most important in applying this aspect of the Ezekiel siege lesson is our need to recognize the value of the right kind of hammering away or repetition in our praying.

Some Christians unfortunately misunderstand the words of Jesus when He told His disciples not to use "vain repetitions" (Matt. 6:7, KJV). We recall He added, "...as the heathen do" (KJV). Jesus was speaking of pagan worshippers who prayed repetitious prayers outside His name and power. In other words, they were praying "empty" (vain) prayers and thus had no basis for authority in their praying.

A specific example might be the Tibetan Buddhists who spin wheels of prayer, each inscribed with the names of hundreds of demonic gods. They believe that each time the wheel spins, a prayer rises to each of the inscribed gods. Obviously, such prayer involves "empty" (meaningless) repetition.

What Jesus did not say was that His followers should never repeat a prayer. Even Jesus prayed five times for the same thing, that His disciples would be "one," in His priestly prayer of John 17. To pray one day for a particular unreached people group to be evangelized, for example, and then pray a similar or even identical prayer the next day is hardly *vain* repetition. Such praying with faith and fervency fits well the battering-ram example of Ezekiel's siege model.

5. Set Up a Wall of Iron Between You and It!

The prophet is finally instructed to raise up a wall of iron, or spiritual shield of protection, between him and his hand-drawn map. Perhaps this was something of a symbolic picture of protection that his prophetic act was to accomplish on behalf of the eventual archers or warriors who would attack the city physically.

Applied to today's battle plan for cities, nations and the lost in general, more intercessors are needed to help shield those serving as frontline vanguards in these battles. Intercessors, likewise, need this kind of prayer protection and thus should seek out their own "covering" as well as pray faithfully for other intercessors they know by name. A most encouraging trend in the church today is the number of pastors and leaders who are recognizing the value of a need to establish personal prayer teams that cover them faithfully in prayer.

In Colorado Springs, Colorado, Bernhard Kuiper, pastor of the large Village Seven Presbyterian Church, has sought to mobilize twenty-eight assigned intercessors to cover each of their several pastors regularly in prayer. The goal is for each of these pastors to meet with seven of his twenty-eight intercessors for a time of prayer at least once a week. Thus, the pastors meet with all twenty-eight of their designated intercessors once a month.

No doubt this is one of the reasons this unique church is having so significant an impact on the Colorado Springs community. These intercessors have, in a sense, helped raise up a "wall of iron" between their pastors and enemy forces that would seek to hinder the ministry potential of this important local church.

Physical Acts in Spiritual Warfare

Interestingly, Ezekiel's unusual act of obedience in laying siege to a hand-drawn map of clay is but one example in Scripture where physical acts of a spiritual nature were somehow linked to the unfolding of God's plans in supernatural ways to accomplish His purposes.

Judah's King Hezekiah came under the verbal attack of the evil King Sennacherib who wrote Hezekiah a letter condemning the God of Israel and the king's capacity to carry out God's plan victoriously. Hezekiah took the accusing letter and spread it before the Lord in a physical act of prayer (2 Kin. 19:8-19). He apparently believed his act of authority in the physical realm would somehow release something of God's presence and provision into the invisible realm resulting in victory.

Hezekiah's spreading of the letter before God obviously was not to let God know he had received a nasty letter. God knew the contents even before Sennacherib's scribe ever set his pen to the parchment. Rather, Hezekiah's act was a physical display of trust that helped establish a foundation for faith upon which he could now bring his petition. The king was so convinced God would hear his prayer that he humbly held the letter before God as a symbol of confidence.

The record indicates Hezekiah's impassioned entreaty resulted in the Lord's sending but a single angel that very night to destroy 185,000 enemy troops (see 2 Kin. 19:35; Is. 37:14-20,36).

Sometimes the Lord actually commanded that a physical act be performed before he would intervene. To Ezekiel He said:

Pound your fists and stamp your feet, and say, "Alas, for all the evil abominations of the house of Israel!" For they shall fall by the sword, by famine, and by pestilence (Ezek. 6:11).

God then told Ezekiel that if he would obey Him in this act, the people would not only know the Lord and His power, but they would go forth to remove all the satanic idols from their altars.

One of Scripture's most unique examples of how a physical act was to impact the supernatural occurred between King Joash and the dying prophet Elisha. During the illness that would eventually take the prophet's life, King Joash visited Elisha and wept over him because of his condition (2 Kin. 13:14). Suddenly, with a burst of energy Elisha commanded the king to take a bow and several arrows into his hand (2 Kin. 13:15). Joash promptly responded and waited for further instructions.

Elisha then directed the king to take the bow and shoot one of the arrows out the window. He explained that the arrow was a picture of the Lord's deliverance for King Joash and God's people and that it would soon be necessary for the king to strike the Syrians until they were destroyed.

Elisha next instructed the king to take the remaining arrows and begin striking them on the ground as a symbolic gesture of his upcoming warfare against the Syrians. Joash obeyed by striking the ground three times (2 Kin. 13:18).

But rather than commending Joash for his obedience, Elisha was angered by the king's apparent lack of authority and intensity in his actions:

You should have struck five or six times; then you would have struck Syria till you had destroyed it! (2 Kin. 13:19).

Elisha was no doubt troubled because Joash did not demonstrate a passionate desperation in his response. Apparently, the Lord was looking for a physical act that manifested an intensity more in keeping with the severity of the challenge.

The Fish and the "For Sale" Sign

Spontaneous physical acts of desperation when accompanied by prayer may sometimes prove essential to the releasing of a long-sought blessing. One such memorable instance occurred with the selling of our home in Southern California just prior to our ministry's move to Colorado Springs.

At the time, the bottom had just fallen out of the local real estate market. I recalled Joshua's leading of the people of Israel across the Jordan River into their land of promise. Their journey couldn't have come at a worse time seasonally — when the river was at its highest. We, too, could not have picked a worse time to move.

Our home went on the market in mid-November, and not a single offer had come four months later. The situation seemed hopeless. The streets of our small community thirty miles north of Los Angeles were lined with "for sale" signs, sometimes representing three and four houses in a row.

It was now Saturday, April 14. I had agreed to drive a large rental truck to our older daughter's college apartment in a distant part of Los Angeles to help her move some of her furniture back home just prior to her college graduation. We planned to drop off several items at our home and then drive three hours south to San Diego with a few pieces of furniture our younger daughter had claimed for her college apartment there. It was going to be a long day.

Gazing with disappointment at the "for sale" sign, I drove the large truck out of our driveway and waited for my wife to follow me in our car. Would we ever find a buyer, I wondered? I'm sure we had prayed at least a hundred times for our house to sell but to no avail.

Looking intently at a sign that had stood fruitless for four months, I suddenly realized I had yet to demonstrate any real desperation regarding this issue. I immediately ruled out doing something similar to what I had read in the newspaper a few weeks earlier. Apparently, certain Roman Catholics in East Los Angeles, in hopes of speeding up the process of selling their homes, had planted small statues of St. Christopher beside their "for sale" signs.

Ridiculous, I thought, noticing Dee was now ready to depart. Still, as I pulled the truck into the street, I couldn't erase the thought from my mind that I had yet to take a bold step to "break" whatever might be keeping the right buyer from discovering our house.

Entering the freeway, a thought flashed through my mind. Our "for sale" sign needed to be anointed with oil. Oil, after all, was a biblical symbol of the Holy Spirit, God's agent for carrying out His plans on earth. Surely God's Spirit could bring just the right buyer to our home.

Feeling somewhat awkward about taking this strange step, I decided not to tell Dee and instead do it alone as soon as possible.

We arrived at our daughter's campus apartment shortly and by noon had loaded the truck. Dee suggested we all have lunch. I thought it best to let them eat without me while I returned home to unload those items not being taken to our other daughter in San Diego.

"By the time you finish eating and get home, I'll probably be ready to drive to San Diego," I said. Deep within, I was thinking about having a few extra minutes to anoint the "for sale" sign with oil, unnoticed. I just couldn't get it out of my mind.

An hour later I was back home and rushed into the house looking for some sort of oil that might qualify for the task. Olive oil was nowhere to be found, but on a shelf filled with spices was a tall bottle of sesame seed oil. Oil is oil, I thought as I grabbed the bottle.

I felt a little odd walking across our driveway heading toward the "for sale" sign clutching a somewhat conspicuous bottle of sesame-seed oil. It was actually huge. But by now I was driven by the reality that we really needed a miracle. Only the Holy Spirit acting on the Father's behalf could possibly bring that much-needed buyer. We had, after all, tried about everything else for more than sixteen weeks, and nothing had happened.

Covering my finger with oil, I drew the outline of a cross on the sign and then prayed. It wasn't a long prayer: "Holy Spirit, I ask You to bring Your perfect choice of just the right buyer to our house in Your perfect timing. Amen!"

I headed back toward the front door. Suddenly I felt an urge to anoint everything in sight with oil, including the huge entry pillars to our home, the front door itself and even our large wooden fish (the sign of a believer). An artist had carved the fish for us, and we had placed it on the front of our home near the entryway.

I returned the bottle of oil to the cupboard and unloaded the items not intended for delivery to San Diego. I had almost finished when my wife arrived. Our older daughter, Dena, had decided to stay with some friends at the campus for a few hours and wouldn't be going with us to San Diego. She'd be home later that evening, Dee explained. We finished unloading the remaining items and soon were on our way to our younger daughter Ginger's apartment three hours south in San Diego. I said nothing to Dee of my sesame-seed-oil adventure as we drove.

We arrived by mid-afternoon and busily unloaded the rental truck. The task was finished by 7:00 P.M. Just as we were about to leave for a quick bite to eat, the phone rang. It was our daughter Dena. She had just arrived home from her last-minute visit with friends at the college and noticed four separate messages on our answer phone. Her voice was filled with both excitement and panic.

"Dad," she exclaimed, "there are four messages on the answering machine — all of them from a realtor! He sounds desperate. He wants to talk to you tonight. He says he's afraid someone else might want to buy our house before his client at least has a chance to make an offer."

I took down his phone number and told our daughter I would call him immediately. A few moments later, I was talking with the realtor explaining we were in San Diego and couldn't possibly arrive home before midnight. We agreed to meet that following afternoon.

A day later, as the realtor sat across from us, I determined not to tell him his was the first and only offer we'd received in four months. He began by saying, "You know, Mr. Eastman, I can't believe how I found your house for my clients. They live quite a distance away in the San Gabriel Valley, but they've been interested in this area for some time. In fact, they actually selected a house just a mile or so from here. Yesterday they decided to make their final offer on that home and had made an appointment with me to help them close the deal.

"As I was waiting for the couple to arrive," he continued, "something prompted me to check my computer one last time for all the listings of homes in their price range. Your home just suddenly appeared on my screen. Although I noticed it had been listed for several months, this was the first time I remember seeing it in my listings."

He paused briefly and then added, "My eyes immediately caught the words 'many bookcases.' Well, my client collects rare books, and he had specifically asked me to look for a house with lots of bookcases. I just hadn't discovered anything quite like this until yesterday."

I knew the realtor had no idea I had taken sesame seed oil and anointed practically everything in sight the day before, including the "for sale" sign, the entryway and even the big wooden fish hanging out front.

The realtor explained his client's offer, hesitating briefly to mention there was one particular contingency that he didn't quite understand.

"I don't know why they would insist on this," the broker said, "but my buyers told me their offer was contingent on the big wooden fish remaining on the house!"

Dee and I instantly realized these buyers had to be believers, remembering how we had often asked God to send some of His followers to buy our house. Later we would learn the buyers of our home were indeed committed Christians who also had prayed that God would lead them to just the right house. And that's exactly what happened. Most interestingly, it had all occurred the very day both the "fish" and the "for sale" sign had been anointed with oil. ❧

TEN

A PROMISE
TO MOSCOW

Personal Encounters With
Prophetic Intercession

PAUL ILYIN, Every Home for Christ's coordinator for the Soviet Union, had experienced a bird's-eye view of the Soviet coup attempt that took place the third week of August 1991. For several days, the fate of the Soviet Union seemed to hang in the balance. Seventy-two hours passed as no one knew for certain whether the communist hard-liners would again gain control of the government or whether there would be a victory leading to an even greater openness for the communication of the gospel.

Early that Monday morning Paul had been awakened by army tanks rolling into Parliament Square. They had been ordered into the heart of the city by communist hard-liners. From Paul's vantage point he could easily see the Russian Parliament Building just across the Volga River. Crowds were beginning to gather by the thousands in opposition to the conspirators.

Interestingly, Paul was in Moscow that very weekend. He was making final preparations for the arrival of more than ten tons of Every Home for Christ gospel messages that were to be used in launching the first-ever, systematic, house-to-house evangelistic coverage of greater Moscow. Five hundred thousand homes were to be targeted initially.

It was a dramatic spiritual confrontation. Just as EHC trucks were being loaded with life-saving "paper missionaries" for the journey from Minsk to Moscow, a satanically inspired coup was commencing in the Soviet Crimea. The then Soviet leader Mikhail Gorbachev was facing the threat of execution. It was almost as if Satan were making a last-ditch effort to stop God's plans for the systematic evangelization of one of the world's most strategic cities.

As these events unfolded, I couldn't erase from my mind a most unusual personal encounter that had happened to me the previous January during my first visit to Moscow. Somehow, these two events now appeared related. On that earlier occasion, a prayer experience had occurred which I'm now convinced contained a clear prophetic picture of what was to happen that following summer on those three tense days.

It was to remind me that any believer, when moving into a position of warfare prayer for others, may well be led into the role of prophetic intercession.

I had been invited to Moscow that January by the International Bible Society which was preparing a massive distribution of four million New Testaments in the Russian language. IBS was graciously making available tens of thousands of those testaments for Every Home for Christ to use in its planned follow-up of new converts once our house-to-house campaign began across the nation. I had been asked to represent the EHC ministry and explain to other mission leaders our plans for the use of these Scriptures in EHC's overall plan.

Little did I know that God would use this occasion to lead me into one of those unusual and rare "vision" experiences of life. It occurred during my final day in Moscow. My plane wasn't scheduled to depart until late that night, and the hotel manager had permitted me to stay in my room throughout the entire day at no extra cost. I realized God was orchestrating my schedule to allow me this special opportunity to seek Him regarding His plans for this crucial Russian city.

I had begun this special time of prayer as I often do, sitting with my Bible in my lap and my feet propped up on the hotel-room bed. As I was praying, I felt a rather overwhelming sense that this casual posture really didn't reflect a particular earnestness of the challenge on my part regarding the ultimate reaching of this city for Jesus — the real purpose for which I had come. It was as if the Lord were whispering in my ear, "Are you really serious about this?"

I thought again of Joshua before the victory of Jericho and how his point of desperate surrender prompted him to fall on his face before his Commander, Christ Himself. Instantly I identified with Joshua as I slipped from my chair and placed myself prostrate on the floor, my face resting in my open Bible. In retrospect I suppose I had anticipated some burst of emotion or at least a feeling of divine destiny. Instead I had a strange sense of emptiness.

A thought that seemed to be of a heavenly origin immediately flooded my mind: "Cry out to God for the city!" I wondered if the Lord was speaking or if my mind was merely looking for a logical next step for my rather dull feelings in prayer. I decided to do exactly what my mind was thinking. Scarcely raising my voice, I prayed a rather tentative prayer: "O Lord, I cry out to You for the salvation of Moscow."

I didn't realize how empty my words had been. Suddenly I knew God was speaking: "Do you seriously call that crying out to Me?"

I couldn't believe how weak my words had been. Still on my face I spoke just a little louder. I still felt inhibited, no doubt by the realization that I was in a hotel room in a foreign country — you just don't cry out to God very loud in such settings.

Then, before I was able to raise my voice any louder, I felt a firm question: "Are you really serious about the lost in this city?"

I responded as positively as I knew how, explaining to the Lord that I truly longed to see all of Moscow reached with the gospel.

What happened next was both unusual and moving. "If you are really serious," I felt the Lord say, "I want you to go to the window, open it and shout a promise to the city that you will be a part of seeing the good news come to every person in Moscow."

By now those earlier empty feelings were gone, and my heart was stirred to action. I stood and moved to the window. I opened it hastily and gasped for air as a rigid rush of arctic cold swept into the room. The outside temperature was 30 degrees below zero.

My heart impressions then became even more specific: "If you are serious about the salvation of this city, I want you to shout a promise to each of these dwellings declaring that you will be a part of helping to bring the good news to every one of them."

Looking out over a vast array of towering high-rise apartment dwellings, I almost felt like thanking God for allowing communist leaders to place the majority of their populations in such concentrated structures. This, I thought, would make it so much easier for us to reach them all, very quickly, with the good news.

I felt an urge to reach out my hand toward each huge complex as far as I could see. Some of them, I was certain, housed thousands of people.

Each time I reached my hands toward a different dwelling I would say, "I promise you — we will bring you the good news."

How long this continued, I do not recall, although the room was becoming colder by the minute. It seemed that scores of apartment buildings providing shelter for thousands of Russian families were visible from the window. The promises were many, and hope was flooding my heart.

I finally shut the window and started to step back when I felt strangely impressed to remain at the closed window. Although my eyes were open and gazing out at scores of high-rise dwellings, I suddenly experienced one of the few, clear "heart" visions of my Christian experience.

Of course, I've come to recognize over the years that a few believers, usually depending on their theological perspective, sometimes have a struggle with the term *vision* when applied to today's context of Christian experience. To these, I've found myself sometimes jokingly suggesting that God simply gave me a "dynamic mental impression." No matter how one might define what happened, I knew that my inner eyes were catching a glimpse of something I could never have imagined on my own.

I could see the army of our Lord accompanied by a multitude of warring intercessors coming from the heavenlies sweeping into the city of Moscow. The Bright Morning Star, Christ Himself, led the charge. They had come to destroy the red star of communism and its seat of authority. It was a direct confrontation between the Bright Morning Star and the communist red star, the symbol of atheistic Leninism that had gripped the region for seventy years.

My mind was picturing a real battle. I felt as if I were an eyewitness to history. I thought of the outbreak of the Persian Gulf War only a few days earlier. For the first time in history, the beginning of a war was televised live by journalists who were eyewitnesses to the conflict. They were watching history happen and reporting it "live" to the entire world.

The one difference between our experiences was that they could not see the eventual outcome of the war. In my heart I was an eyewitness to a spiritual battle against a powerful stronghold that I was sure was about to fall. I felt I was seeing the outcome before it actually happened. My heart was filled with the impression, "There is a miracle coming to this city, and the red star of communism will be destroyed."

Returning home, I wrote a magazine article that I chose to title "A Promise to Moscow." It was published the following month. In it I described this unique prophetic encounter and the impression that a miracle was coming to Moscow. I couldn't explain the miracle but felt it would spell the defeat of the red star of communism. I had no idea what was destined to happen just a few months later in August.

When I awakened on Monday, August 19, 1991, my heart sank as I heard the news. An attempted coup was underway in the Soviet Union. Hard-line communist leaders had initiated it, and the outcome was in doubt. Concern filled our hearts for our Russian coordinator who was to be in Moscow that very day to launch our first-ever Moscow Every Home Crusade. Now it seemed all might be lost.

Could I have been wrong about my impressions of the red star of communism being smashed in Moscow, impressions that had come eight months earlier during my first visit to the city?

I now believe that during those following three days a powerful assault was orchestrated by the armies of heaven against the controlling forces of Satan over Moscow and the entire Soviet Union. God's people everywhere were praying. And within seventy-two hours the red star of communism had indeed taken a direct hit.

By Friday, September 6, 1991, just sixteen days after the coup ended, the headline on the front page of *USA Today* would read: "The Soviet Union Is Finished." By that December the break-up of the Soviet Union would be complete. It would, interestingly, be finalized on Christmas Day.

Few people could have imagined in late August 1991 that by the following February, just five months after the coup, the Soviet national anthem would not be played at the Winter Olympics in France. Nor would their once-proud national flag fly, even when an athlete from the region was awarded a gold medal.

The Soviet Union simply no longer existed. Minsk was even being discussed as the possible future capital city for the newly formed Commonwealth of Independent States.

Most amazing to me about those three days in August 1991 were the spiritual implications for the ministry of Every Home for Christ. Our Soviet Union coordinator, Paul Ilyin, had been but a stone's throw from the Russian Parliament when the tanks rolled across the Volga River that bleak Monday morning. At the same time our trucks loaded with literature had been scheduled to arrive from Minsk with ten tons of life-giving gospel messages for the families of Moscow. But the trucks were kept out as the tanks moved in.

Then, three days later, when the coup failed, the tanks were forced out, and our trucks promptly moved in. By week's end the first twenty thousand homes of Moscow's inhabitants had each been visited by a small band of initial crusade workers. Within sixteen months, over two million dwellings (many I had seen from my hotel room eighteen months earlier) were visited. This resulted in over a hundred thousand written decision cards being received in our Moscow office and at least thirty new home-church fellowships planted throughout greater Moscow.

Other ministries have discovered equally fertile soil. Campus Crusade for Christ's *JESUS* film has been seen by millions, and tens of thousands of once Soviet citizens have met Christ. The Christian Broadcasting Network has broadcast television spots about Jesus freely throughout the fifteen republics resulting in several million inquiries.

The Co-Mission formed as a networking strategy of scores of ministries committed to impacting the public school system of the old Soviet Union. That united effort and others like it have responded to a Russian invitation to send trained Christian teachers to teach Christian principles of morality and ethics to their young people.

Billy Graham has preached to huge crowds in Moscow and repeatedly shouted "don't run" to thousands jamming the aisles in response to the evangelist's invitations. In one Graham rally, the Russian army choir sang phonetically in English *The Battle Hymn of the Republic* by Julia Ward Howe. No believer a decade ago could ever have imagined the Russian army choir singing these words at a Moscow-wide Billy Graham crusade:

> In the beauty of the lilies Christ was born across the sea
> With glory in His bosom that transfigures you and me;
> As He died to make men holy, let us live to make men
>   free;
> While God is marching on.

Understanding Prophetic Intercession

My Moscow experience on a freezing-cold January day in 1991 provided a unique personal encounter with prophetic intercession. Frankly, I had never really understood this subject, let alone experienced it at such a dimension. In fact, I usually questioned those who spoke too much of the prophetic dimension, because it seemed to be an area vulnerable to excess. But I soon learned an important lesson: whenever any sensitive intercessor moves into a prolonged season of intercessory prayer, there is the potential for God to use that person to pray prophetically.

Quite often, the intercessor will not realize this is happening. If the person does, he or she will recognize that what is being prayed has originated with God. They are, in a sense, praying a "word" from the Lord. Jeremiah's calling to the role of a prophetic intercessor, cited in an earlier chapter, contains a variety of insights that help us understand this role (see Jer. 1:4-10).

Jeremiah's age and inexperience (a youth no doubt filled with many fears and insecurities) serve to remind us that any available believer of almost any age (capable of comprehending the ways of God) can be an intercessor who is moved at times to pray prophetically.

Upon receiving his calling, Jeremiah promptly informs the Lord, "I cannot speak, for I am a youth" (Jer. 1:6).

And the Lord replies firmly:

Do not say "I am a youth"...Do not be not afraid of their
faces, for I am with you to deliver you (Jer. 1:7-8).

Following this promise, the Lord touched Jeremiah's lips, declaring, "Behold, I have put My words in your mouth" (Jer. 1:9).

Interestingly, some of the words God put in Jeremiah's mouth
were not performed until well after his death. Yet nothing the Lord
spoke to Jeremiah was left undone. He was both a prophet and an
intercessor. Indeed, a careful look at all the prophets of Scripture
would indicate that each one fulfilled the role of intercessor as well
as prophet. They stepped into the battle of others as intercessors
through the words God put in their mouths as prophets.

In her widely read book *Possessing the Gates of the Enemy, Cindy
Jacobs defines prophetic intercession as "an urging to pray given by
the Holy Spirit for situations or circumstances about which you have
very little knowledge in the natural. You pray for the prayer requests
that are on the heart of God. God will direct you to pray to bring forth
His will on the earth as it is willed in heaven."*[1]

Cindy explains further that prophetic intercessors, those with a
special gift of intercession, actually prophesy as they pray. Regarding the role of the prophetic, she notes C. Peter Wagner's definition
of prophecy from his widely read study Your Spiritual Gifts Can
Help Your Church Grow.

> The gift of prophecy is the special ability God gives to
> certain members of the body of Christ to receive and
> communicate an immediate message of God to His peo-
> ple through a divinely anointed utterance.[2]

Applying this definition to prophetic intercession, Cindy explains:

> We could adapt this to say that the gift of prophetic
> intercession is the ability to receive an immediate prayer
> request from God and pray about it in a divinely
> anointed utterance.[3]

In the context of Christ's revelation to John and the invitation
that goes forth to Christ's bride to come to the marriage supper of
the Lamb, we discover an interesting phrase: "For the testimony of

123

Jesus is the spirit of prophecy" (Rev. 19:10). Of this passage Jack Hayford explains:

> The entire Bible is a product of the Holy Spirit, who is not only "the Spirit of truth" (John 16:13), but "the spirit of prophecy" (Rev. 19:10). The verb "to prophesy" (derived from the Greek preposition *pro* and verb *pehmi*) means "to speak from before." The preposition "before" in this use may mean: 1) "in advance" and/or 2) "in front of." Thus, *to prophesy* is a proper term to describe the proclamation of God's Word as it forecasts events. It may also describe the declaration of God's Word forthrightly, boldly, or confrontingly before a group of individuals — telling forth God's truth and will. So, in both respects, the Bible is prophetic: a Book that reveals God's will through His Word and His words, as well as a Book that reveals God's plans and predictions.[4]

From this definition we see that prophecy is not only to speak something *before* it happens. It is also to stand before a group of people (or even before a particular circumstance or obstacle) and, by the power of the Holy Spirit, make a prophetic declaration of God's intended will regarding that group, circumstance or obstacle. No doubt this is what transpired when God commissioned His prophets in ancient days to stand before the mountains and speak His words to them (see Ezek. 6:2; 36:1; Mic. 6:1).

There are, indeed, occasions when intercessors are used in prayer to speak a declaration of God's intended will regarding a situation *before* it happens. In fact, in some cases a prophetic prayer may be essential to the release of the very answer sought. A vivid example comes to mind regarding the move of Every Home for Christ from Southern California to Colorado Springs.

Prophetic Prayer: an Example

For weeks EHC staff members had been praying for the sale of our headquarters in an industrial area of the city. Now it was six weeks into the new year, and the projected move of the ministry that summer grew more and more uncertain without a firm offer from someone to purchase our property.

It was our EHC day of prayer for the month of February, a day that began not unlike any of our usual monthly days of prayer. Eight years earlier I had decided to set aside one day a month to spend with local intercessors and staff who would unite in providing a prayer covering for our ministry as well as others laboring to evangelize a lost world.

We had begun at 8:30 A.M. and for almost ninety minutes had prayed for a variety of needs, many representing those EHC families who planned to move with us to Colorado but were having difficulty selling their homes. Soon the sale of the EHC office building had become the focus. The prayers were all sincere, but nothing of a particular intensity in the praying caught my attention. Most were simply asking God to intervene in the difficult economic climate that prevailed throughout the area.

What happened next prompted me to look at my watch. It was 9:55 A.M. One of the intercessors who had been petitioning God for His intervention had completely changed the tone of his praying. He had been rehearsing in prayer certain factors God was certainly well aware of: the declining economic conditions of the city; recent articles in the local newspaper explaining how few, if any, office buildings were selling in the Los Angeles area; and the fact that our small street was lined with buildings for sale, some perhaps better and even cheaper than ours. What a faith-building prayer!

But then came the change. The prayer seemed to take a quantum spiritual leap in boldness. It began with a simple phrase, "God, no matter the circumstance, You have just the right buyer for this building." Next came, "In fact, I believe You can see that buyer even now. You know his name. You can see where he is — what he's doing right now."

What happened next I believe was a divinely initiated transition into the arena of prophetic prayer. The intercessor suddenly spoke directly to the would-be buyer: "I believe that even now God sees you driving along the streets near the EHC office looking for just the right building for your business." An even more startling directive followed: "I command you to come forth now. Not tomorrow, not next week, not next month, but today."

There was a hush in the room. This was no ordinary generalized prayer. It was about as measurable as any prayer could be. Everyone present was aware God knew who the buyer might be and exactly where he was at the time. But we also knew the building had been on the market for many months, and not a single offer had come.

In the silence no one seemed to know how to follow up such an audacious prayer. Finally, someone graciously began speaking praises into the hushed room, as one of our staff stood to leave for another commitment. She was gone only moments when she re-entered the room and came over to my side. My eyes closed in prayer, I was momentarily startled as she tapped me on the shoulder.

"Dick," she whispered, "I thought you'd like to know that just as I walked from the prayer room past the receptionist, an older man with a young couple walked in the front door. They said they were just driving in the area looking for available buildings and saw our 'for sale' sign. They apologized for not having an appointment and wondered if someone could show them around."

I looked again at my watch. It was a few minutes past 10:00 A.M. Inwardly, I wondered if this was merely a coincidence or the start of a miracle.

Today, the full story is known. The elderly man was the owner of a family business, and the young man and woman were his children. They, indeed, had been driving throughout the San Fernando Valley that morning looking for a possible new site for expanding their business.

At the exact moment the prophetic prayer had begun in our prayer room, they turned onto our side street from a main thoroughfare crossing that part of the valley. At 10:00 A.M., they stopped their car in front of our office and walked in. Theirs would be the only offer ever made on the property. In fact, I cannot recall any others even coming to look at the building.

The price would be everything we could have hoped for in the economic conditions of the season. The purchase was finalized exactly on time for that summer's move to Colorado Springs. And it had all begun with a prophetic prayer! ⌛

ELEVEN

ONCE AND
FOR ALL

Closing in on "Closure"
of the Great Commission

I SAT straight up in bed and broke out in a cold sweat. It was a cool, misty night in Japan. At first I thought it was just another jet-lag awakening. I had been in Japan less than forty-eight hours, preparing for a nationwide congress on prayer and evangelism.

Suddenly I realized I had been awakened by a word from the Lord — actually four powerful, prophetic words. The words echoed repeatedly in my mind. *"Once and for all!"* I knew it was God stirring my heart regarding His commission to disciples everywhere to take the good news of His Son "once and for all" to the ends of the earth.

Two years earlier I had inherited the leadership of Every Home for Christ, a world evangelism ministry committed to taking a printed message of the gospel to every home on earth. It had been founded by Jack McAlister, a Canadian pastor and radio preacher who had been greatly influenced by missionary statesman Oswald J. Smith. Smith had reportedly often declared, "Why should anyone hear the gospel twice when millions have never heard it once?" I thought of this powerful statement of Smith's as the words "once and for all" saturated my mind.

It was very fitting that God would speak these words to me in Japan. It was in Japan in the early 1900s when the first twentieth-century plan would emerge with a goal of taking the gospel, systematically, to every creature. Here, in the land of the rising sun, Charles and Lettie Cowman became burdened to reach "every creature" using literature as the primary means. They soon established an Every Creature Crusade that was to begin in Japan. (Years later, God used the Cowmans to birth two ministries, Oriental Missionary Society and World Gospel Crusades.

Charles Cowman did not live beyond 1924 but survived to see every identifiable village of Japan reached before his death. It required many difficult years. His wife, Lettie, later became best known for authoring one of the century's most beloved devotional classics, *Streams in the Desert*. The book was born out of long days and sleepless nights as she ministered to her dying husband.

Literature distribution was at the heart of the Cowmans' Every Creature Crusade, but illiteracy was a significant challenge in those early years, especially in many remote villages. Still, the Cowmans launched similar campaigns in several countries over the ensuing years, a vision Lettie Cowman sustained for some four decades after Charles's death.

It was also in Japan, half a century after the Cowmans' first Japanese crusade, that a young Canadian radio preacher, with a passionate conviction to send literature to the ends of the earth, received a renewed vision to reach every person on earth with the gospel, systematically, right where they lived.

Jack McAlister had founded the Radio Tract Club of the Air in 1946 in Prince Albert, Saskatchewan. For almost six years he had encouraged the mass distribution of the printed page by missionaries and laymen throughout the world. Then, while on a visit to Japan in 1952, Jack became convinced there was only one way to ensure that all people of a nation have a reasonable opportunity to know about Christ: take a printed message of the gospel to where they lived. The first Every Home Crusade was born.

During the next four decades, these systematic campaigns touched nation after nation until more than 147 nations had experienced an Every Home Crusade, and 66 nations, including the massive land of India, had been completely covered at least once.

This book has focused mainly on strategic-level prayer, but we must not forget that the ultimate focus of all such prayer is the harvest. True, there may be focuses of a strategic nature that may not appear to touch the lost directly, such as fervent prayer for the peace of a war-torn region of the world or the health of a missionary ravaged by a life-threatening illness. But when you examine the ultimate impact of those prayers the harvest is still the primary issue. Peace in that troubled region would mean opportunity to evangelize more freely, and healing for the missionary could mean the continuation of a productive soul-saving ministry. Both could have a great deal to do with closure, and, thus, both could be very strategic.

Just how close are we to closure? With the uniting of scores of missionary agencies and denominations under such banners as the AD 2000 and Beyond Movement and the Lausanne Committee for World Evangelization, the question of ultimate closure of the Great Commission is increasingly on the minds of missiologists and other church leaders alike. Could this be the generation that finally witnesses the climax of Christ's commission to His church and closure regarding the matter of global evangelization? If so, what will it take to evangelize the world? I believe the answer is embodied in at least three primary or unalterable convictions.

An Obedient Church

First, if the world is to be evangelized in our generation, *the Great Commission must be taken literally by believers everywhere.* Scripture convinces us the whole world can and will be evangelized. It is merely a matter of time before a particular generation of committed believers finally obeys the Lord and accomplishes the task — fully.

The scope of the commission is seen clearly in Christ's words. In Matthew 28:19 we read, "Go therefore and make disciples of all the nations." Note the word *all*. In Mark's record we read, "Go into all the world and preach the gospel to every creature" (Mark 16:15). Note *all* and *every*. Some scholars have brought into question the validity of quoting these closing words of Mark's Gospel because of their absence in some early New Testament Greek texts. But it is very clear from other passages of Scripture that God clearly wills that every person on earth has access to the gospel — personally.

Peter wrote:

> The Lord is not slack concerning His promise, as some count slackness, but is longsuffering toward us, not willing that any should perish but that all should come to repentance (2 Pet. 3:9).

To young Timothy, Paul also stressed the scope of God's intent regarding the ultimate communication of the gospel. Paul pleads for prayers of intercession on behalf of "all men," especially "for kings and all who are in authority." He adds:

> For this is good and acceptable in the sight of God our Savior, who desires all men to be saved and to come to the knowledge of the truth (1 Tim. 2:1-4).

But is it reasonable to believe that all of this could be accomplished in our generation? Never has the church been filled with more hope in addressing this question. Ministries involved in frontline evangelism, such as Every Home for Christ, Campus Crusade for Christ, Youth With a Mission and Operation Mobilization, along with numerous denominations with aggressive missions programs, have reported remarkable increases in response to their efforts over the past three years. Denominational and interdenominational church-planting strategies (like DAWN — Discipling A Whole Nation) also are experiencing significant progress.

It is especially encouraging to note an emerging trend in world evangelism: The printed page is becoming recognized as a powerful means to present the gospel systematically to an entire people group or nation. Under the banner of the AD 2000 and Beyond Movement, a specialized "track" or coalition of like-minded ministries has been formed called the God's Word and Literature Track, increasingly being referred to by track participants simply as GWALT.

The goal of GWALT is to network Bible societies and literature-evangelism ministries along with mission mobilizers in a strategic plan to take the salvation message to an entire nation. They would do this by partnering together in a campaign to visit every home or dwelling in a nation and provide each home's inhabitants with a clear message of the gospel, whether printed or recorded.

Although ministries like Every Home for Christ have long sought to do just this, there were always too many harvest fields and too few workers or resources to accomplish the task. That may be changing, along with the growing recognition that literature evangelism, if done systematically and with recorded messages for illiterates, could be the quickest way to evangelize a nation in a *truly measurable manner.*

Exactly how significant is literature in evangelism? Patrick Johnstone, author of the definitive intercessor's guide *Operation World,* points out that half of all the Christians in the world testify that literature played a major role in their conversion.[1]

Ralph Winter, founder of the U.S. Center for World Mission, goes even further.

> There are two things in the entire history of missions that have been absolutely central. The one, most obviously, is the Bible itself. The other is the printed page. There is absolutely nothing else in terms of missions methodology that outranks the importance of the printed page. Meetings come and go. Personalities appear and are gone. But the printed page continues to speak.[2]

Frank Gaebelein, a former editor of *Christianity Today,* wrote:

> Among the eternal resources available to the Church, the printed page stands first.[3]

Of their work among Muslims, Bob Hoskins, founder of Life Publishers, a worldwide publishing ministry, wrote:

> The power of the Gospel is not in a building. It is not in a man. The power of the Gospel is in the Gospel! The

Gospel *is* the power of God unto salvation! The Holy
Spirit does not have a nationality — He embraces *all*
nations! The Holy Spirit is not bound by men's laws and
regulations. He doesn't need a passport. In our ministry
we discovered that wherever we could get the Word of
God in printed form, even without a preacher, the Holy
Spirit would accompany the written word, revealing
Christ in bringing Muslims to a knowledge of a saving
truth.[4]

Bob Hoskins quickly discovered the amazing power of the
printed page in evangelism when he went to the Middle East as a
missionary. He had gone with his wife, Hazel, to Beirut, Lebanon,
in the mid-1960s with a burden to present the gospel to the Arab
population by means of television.

They had initially received permission from the Lebanese government to begin a Christian television program which would have been
the first of its kind in that region of the world. Thousands of dollars
had been raised, and believers back home were excited about the
prospects. The Hoskinses had even produced several telecasts to be
broadcast. Then, without warning, merely hours before the first program was to be aired, an upheaval occurred in the government.
Permission to broadcast the programs was denied. Heartbroken, Bob
and Hazel Hoskins sought God for wisdom.

They soon realized God had another plan to get the good news
to these people in a way that would accomplish the task as effectively as television but wouldn't attract as much attention and
hostility. It was also much less expensive. The Hoskinses felt
directed to print a series of announcements in local Arabic news-
papers offering readers home study courses on how to find fulfillment in life. They also developed a simple set of six Arabic Bible
study lessons, each written in a way to arouse more curiosity.

To their amazement, within just a few months, several thousand
Arabs were enrolled. Before long the number reached a hundred
thousand. Within ten years, more than four hundred thousand
students from twenty-six Arabic-speaking countries had enrolled in
the six-lesson program. No doubt God has planted these precious
descendants of Ishmael (Gen. 16:7-16) throughout these nations
just waiting to blossom into fruition in His perfect timing.

The ministry of Every Home for Christ has seen similar response to the systematic distribution of the printed good news of Jesus Christ globally. By the time our first literature coverage to more than five hundred thousand villages of India was completed after ten years in December 1974, our ten offices in India had already received an amazing 1,250,058 response cards. Each of these respondees had been enrolled in a four-part Bible correspondence course, and by that year already a remarkable 142,477 had finished all four lessons in the course.

Today, those numbers have increased more than fourfold and are resulting in the planting of over five hundred small New Testament fellowships of believers every month (seventeen per day) in villages of India where no churches have previously existed.

Saved by Fire

In many cases, conversions by means of the printed page have been most unique. During our first Every Home Crusade in Japan in the 1950s, a Shinto worshipper was preparing her hibachi for the evening meal. For kindling she decided to use pages of a small pamphlet that had been left at her home by two strange young men who visited her village earlier that day.

Just as she put a match to the booklet, a single word caught her eye. She quickly extinguished the flame and sat down to read the partially scorched message. In moments she felt somewhat like John Wesley who generations earlier had described his heart as being "strangely warmed" when he understood the reality of the gospel. In a matter of moments, the woman was converted.

In Southern Africa, Jacob Phokanoka was in his final days of schooling and seriously questioning his future. He walked from the center of the village where he had been listening to an elderly village leader strumming his guitar. He was looking down as he walked, wondering how well he would do on his exams and what might lie ahead in his life.

Jobs were almost nonexistent, and his family had no money for further education. He later wrote of feeling an unusual restlessness as he walked along that dusty path toward his village nearby. Suddenly, his eyes caught a glimpse of something strange amid the sand and pebbles. He reached to pick it up. It was an old cork with paper wrapped around it. Apparently, someone had used the paper as a means to keep the cork in a bottle. The youth unraveled the paper and discovered that it contained printing in his own Sepedi language.

Much of the message was gone, but one line leaped from the tattered page — "to delay is dangerous — deadly dangerous. It is time to make a decision now. Believe in the Lord Jesus Christ!" The message promised peace if the reader would but believe the message.

Jacob's heart leaped within him. He had to know more. He couldn't explain what he was feeling. Carefully, he deciphered the tiny lettering of an address on the bottom of the page. It was the address of the nearest Every Home Crusade office in Africa. A few days later, a letter from Jacob arrived at the office. Follow-up literature was sent to the young man. By summer's end he was gloriously converted and attending a nearby church.

Bob Hoskins recounts an equally moving story of a ten-year-old girl named María in Chile.[5] María was responsible for doing the cooking and washing for her father following her mother's untimely death. Her father was a miner.

She attended a little community church at the foot of a mountain in Central Chile where she had met Christ some months earlier. After her mother's death María had become increasingly concerned about her father who was growing deeply despondent. She often invited him to go to church and begged him to read the Bible and other Christian literature, but he repeatedly refused.

One night, as María prepared sandwiches for her father's lunch pail, she placed in it a little booklet explaining God's plan of salvation. She prayed a simple prayer that night: "O Jesus, please help my father read this message so that he might be saved."

Her father left late that night to work in the nearby mine. At 1:10 A.M., an explosion shook the small mountain village, and sirens began to echo across the valley floor. María, along with scores of villagers, ran to the mine where workers rushed about frantically. María's father was one of those trapped with a handful of others inside a collapsed shaft.

Workers dug through the crumbling debris throughout the night and into the next day hoping to find survivors. Finally, they reached a chamber where María's father and a group of other miners were located. All had died of suffocation, but the position of the dead miners was most interesting. They were found sitting serenely in a circle — all eight of them.

On the lap of María's father was the small booklet the young girl had placed in her father's lunch pail. It was opened to the last page where the plan of salvation was clearly explained. On it María's father had written a special message to his daughter:

> My darling María, when you read this, I will be with your mother in heaven. I read this little book, then I read it several times to the men while we waited to be rescued. Our hope is faded for this life, but not for the next. We did as the book told us and prayed, asking Jesus into our hearts. I love you very much, María, and one day soon, we will all be together in heaven.

Measuring Closure

Is it possible to measure the progress being made toward closure of the Great Commission? The answer is yes, if by closure we mean providing every person reasonable access to the gospel. Of course, only God knows when the task really will be completed, but there are clear ways we can chart our progress.

Certainly, the printed page and other repeatable means of presenting the message (such as the *JESUS* film) which can be shared over vast areas of the world quickly will be instrumental in this task. But merely distributing the message of the gospel in "shotgun" fashion without having a systematic strategy to assure everyone reasonable access to the message would leave huge pockets of humanity unevangelized.

We also must define what we mean by *evangelized*. The Foreign Mission Board of the Southern Baptist Convention offers this definition:

> A person is evangelized who has heard the gospel of Jesus Christ, of His death, burial, and resurrection in his or her own culture with sufficient understanding to accept or reject Christ.[6]

Lars Dunberg, president of the International Bible Society, advises:

> No people group or nation can be considered evangelized unless they have access to God's Word in their own language.[7]

Luis Bush of the AD 2000 and Beyond Movement would suggest the twofold vision statement of this movement as a good place to begin: "A church for every people. The gospel for every person."

Frank Kaleb Jansen, a former Norwegian naval officer and present executive director of Adopt-a-People Clearing House, wisely suggests five questions we should ask in determining if a people group has been evangelized:

1. Have they received or heard the gospel in a language they can understand?

2. Have they responded to the gospel upon receiving it?

3. Do they have an indigenous, evangelizing church in their midst?

4. Do they have the Word of God, all or portions of it, in a language they can understand?

5. And, finally, is the Word actually available and accessible to them (not just translated into their language)?[8]

Jansen, too, believes the task must be approached systematically. He told a strategic consultation on unreached peoples:

> The word most often translated as "nations" in the Old Testament refers to clans or families. The only way to truly measure the progress of reaching every unreached people group is to go to where they live — in their homes, huts, and dwellings.[9]

Naturally, all that is needed to accomplish these objectives is a willingness of churches, evangelistic agencies, missions, Bible societies, short-term workers, denominations and others involved in evangelism to unify around a simple strategy: we must go where people live — at least once! This makes the task of world evangelization both manageable and measurable. D. L. Moody, speaking of the reality of closure over a century ago, declared, "It can be done; it ought to be done; it must be done."[10]

In 1908 the gifted Bible teacher S. D. Gordon devoted an entire volume of his famed "Quiet Talks" series specifically to world evangelization. In *Quiet Talks for World Winners* he suggested that the task was not as difficult as we made it out to be if we would simply give, pray and unite around a simple plan. He called it "the Master's plan" for world evangelization. Of this plan he wrote:

> The great concern now is to make Jesus fully known to all mankind. That is the plan. It is a simple plan. Men who have been changed are to be world-changers. Nobody else can be. The warm enthusiasm of grateful love must burn in the heart and drive all of one's life. There must be simple, but thorough organization.
>
> The campaign should be mapped out as thoroughly as a presidential campaign is organized in America. The purpose of a presidential campaign is really stupendous in its object and sweep. It is to influence quickly, up to the point of decisive action, the individual opinion of millions of men, spread over millions of square miles, and that, too, in the face of a vigorous opposing campaign to influence them the other way. The whole country is mapped out and organized on broad lines and into the smallest details.
>
> Strong, intelligent men give themselves wholly to the task, and spend tens of millions of dollars within a few months. And then, four years later, they proceed as enthusiastically as before to go over the whole ground again. We need as thorough organizing, as aggressive enthusiasm, and as intelligent planning for this great task our Master has put into our hands.[11]

The Tire-Pump Miracle

Jesus clearly intends for all to be reached with the message of salvation, a lesson one Every Home for Christ field evangelist in India learned in a rather humorous manner.

The worker had been visiting various villages in a particular sector of his assigned region and was now finishing the door-to-door campaign in a small, rural town. He had contacted what appeared to be every home in the village and was preparing to mount his bicycle and head back to the base camp several miles away. There he would join other workers who would be housed for the night.

Preparing to leave, his eyes caught a glimpse of a tiny hut high atop a distant hill he knew he had not visited. His heart sank as he thought about hiking to the top of the hill. But he quickly realized making such a trip might necessitate his spending the night in the village or at least riding his bicycle along miles of unlit path in the dark back to the camp. And, he reasoned, it was only one tiny hut anyway.

Realizing no one saw him but God and trusting the Father's mercy both to forgive him for his neglect as well as send another someday to that distant hut with the gospel, the worker mounted his only means of transportation, a well-worn EHC bicycle.

But clearly something was amiss. The pedals would hardly move. Gazing back at his rear tire, the young evangelist noticed the air had seeped out of the tire while the bicycle had sat idle most of the day.

A few village shops were still open, and the worker began inquiring about the availability of a tire pump. It was a slow leak, he reasoned, and with a little air he could make it to the camp. But it soon became evident no one in the village had a pump. Then, while imagining himself pushing his bicycle several miles in the dark, he saw a small boy heading in his direction.

"Young lad," he questioned, "is there anyone in the village with a bicycle pump?"

The youth gave a prompt but polite reply, "No, I don't believe so," when his eyes suddenly lit up.

"Oh, I just remembered," he said. "There is one old man near this village whom I have seen with a tire pump." He pointed over the shoulder of the evangelist. "If you look carefully you can see his house high on that hill!"

The smile on the weary worker's face seemed to release fresh energy into both his body and spirit as he began climbing the hill.

God is not willing that any should perish, he thought, as he clutched his shoulder bag filled with life-giving messages about Christ.

The old man living in the hut was delighted to have a visitor and even more delighted to have something to read. He no doubt had learned to read years earlier, but literature was scarce. And he had a tire pump and was glad to loan it to the evangelist.

Late in the day when the young man climbed the hill again to return the pump, it occurred to him that God loved this old man enough to require two trips to his hut in one day. God indeed is not willing that any should perish!

A United Church

Our merely acknowledging the scope of the Great Commission and affirming the need for some kind of a systematic strategy to fulfill it is not enough. If the world is to be evangelized fully in our generation, the whole church (that is, all those who believe the truth of God's Word) must unite to finish the task. Stated simply, *without unity, world evangelization is impossible.*

Perhaps this is why Jesus prayed so passionately that His disciples would be one. Indeed, when He offered up His high-priestly prayer (see John 17:17-23), He mentioned this unity at least five times. Twice His petition explained why — "that the world may believe" and "that the world may know" (see John 17:21,23).

Essential to the ultimate fulfilling of the Great Commission will be the networking of perhaps hundreds of ministries and strategies committed to the task. Already, exciting examples of such uniting of efforts provides great encouragement. Following the dramatic open door to the old Soviet Union, Every Home for Christ began developing a plan to launch systematic literature distribution campaigns across the fifteen Soviet republics, beginning with the capital city of each. Moscow, of course, was to be one of the first.

A three-year plan to reach the entire city of Moscow developed and was launched in late August 1991. It was progressing at a moderate pace when the fall 1992 Billy Graham Crusade was scheduled. Word reached some of the crusade planners in Moscow that an effort was underway to visit every home systematically with a gospel message in the city. It was suggested that a simple crusade invitation be added to the normally distributed booklets, inviting people to the meeting.

The linking of these efforts most certainly proved beneficial to

139

the overall results of both efforts. No doubt the EHC-organized door-to-door visits made more Moscow inhabitants aware of the Graham crusade. At the same time, the Graham team's encouragement of the house-to-house campaign drew into the EHC effort many additional churches that might otherwise never have become involved.

The Baptist Union also provided all the paper for the project at a cost equivalent to just five dollars, an amount so low as to be almost free. Through these unified efforts over five hundred thousand homes in the city of Moscow were reached in a few weeks instead of many months. And within ninety days of the Graham campaign, EHC was helping to nurture at least thirty New Testament house fellowships of new believers established as a result of this combined effort.

A similar spirit of unity in ministry has touched a million families in Cuba where World Missionary Press provided one million gospel booklets for an equal number of Cuban families. Every Home for Christ then mobilized the local believers to reach these homes, systematically, over a period of several months. To date, more than ninety thousand people have professed Christ in the overall Cuban campaign in spite of difficulties posed by working in this still communist land.

Another example of a simple cooperative effort occurred between Every Home for Christ and Campus Crusade for Christ in the small Caribbean island of St. Kitts. As EHC targeted the island for home-to-home distribution of gospel literature, pastors informed EHC planners that Campus Crusade was organizing the showing of the highly successful *JESUS* film. It was to be shown in four locations just at the time volunteer workers would be going home-to-home throughout the island.

It was another of God's divine coincidences. Campus Crusade workers provided EHC with nicely printed invitations listing the four showings of the *JESUS* film. EHC added these invitations to the usual gospel booklets and response cards that were to be placed in every dwelling on the island.

In the immediate days following the distribution, more than 650 response cards were returned to the local island address printed on the decision cards. Each person responding was enrolled in a four-part Bible correspondence course. Then Campus Crusade for

Christ, true to its vision, presented the four showings of the *JESUS* film. A thrilling two thousand islanders attended these showings where hundreds publicly professed Christ as Savior.

I'm convinced the impact of these two evangelistic activities in this island nation was considerably enhanced because two ministries united their efforts. And I'm thankful for this spirit of unity that appears to be spreading.

One of the more encouraging signs of emerging unity for world evangelization is such networking strategies as the already mentioned AD 2000 and Beyond Movement. Directed by Luis Bush, an Argentine-born missions strategist, the movement seeks to unite scores of ministries and strategies in direct partnership to fulfill the overall movement's dual vision statement: "A Church for every people. The Gospel for every person." Various special-interest groups representing a variety of evangelistic or research focuses are networked together in like-minded tracks to help them concentrate their efforts.

Many of these tracks are now uniting with one another to serve each other. Both God's Word and Literature Track (GWALT) and the Saturation Evangelism Track (including the *JESUS* film project) are seeking to work alongside the saturation church-planting track, which includes DAWN (Discipling A Whole Nation). The overall goal is the birthing of multitudes of new churches by uniting resources to evangelize a whole nation town by town, block by block and home by home, until the task is accomplished.

But none of this could happen without the top leadership of these numerous ministries and strategies investing their time to enter into prayer relationships with one another to nurture and guard this unity.

Finishing Together

Needed to sustain such unity is a childlike simplicity, the kind demonstrated several years ago at the world's Special Olympics in Los Angeles.

A handful of teenagers stood anxiously at the starting line of a sprint race awaiting the "go" signal. One could tell, even at a distance, that these youths were different from other youngsters. Their minds had not developed much beyond the level of young children.

The starter called them to their mark. His pistol fired, and the field of runners lunged forward. To some it almost appeared as if the race were being run in slow motion. But the teens were doing their best, and each was clearly excited to be there.

Only seconds into the race one of the runners, a girl, tripped and fell helplessly to the track. Her knee hit hard, breaking the skin and releasing a small flow of blood. She reacted as a small child would, screaming in pain as she gripped her knee and rolled into a fetal position.

What happened next amazed everyone. The other participants, hearing the cries of a competitor, stopped. They turned and ran back to her, kneeling at her side while the crowd watched in awe. One of the young men kissed the hurting knee tenderly.

Suddenly, all of the runners, as if acting on some unselfish instinct, picked up the injured youth and put her on their shoulders. Then, as one, they set out to run the race together, crossing the finish line in unison as a tearful crowd cheered them on.

A Praying Church

A final unalterable conviction is especially critical if we're to see closure in the matter of world evangelization in our generation. It's a conviction that has been central to this book. *No obstacle can stand in the way of a praying church.* J. Sidlow Baxter declared:

> Men may spurn our appeals, reject our message, oppose our arguments, despise our persons, but they are helpless against our prayers.[12]

A. T. Pierson adds:

> Generally, if not uniformly, prayer is both starting point and goal to every movement in which are the elements of permanent progress. Wherever the Church is aroused and the world's wickedness is arrested, somebody, somewhere has been praying.[13]

When Jesus looked at a vast harvest field of lost humanity while recognizing the severe scarcity of workers to reach them, He didn't say, "The harvest truly is plenteous, and the laborers are few, build ye therefore bigger and better seminaries and thus thou shalt train more workers!" Nor did He order: "Plan ye therefore worker-mobilization conferences," or "organize ye therefore evangelism awareness seminars."

As good as all of these things may be, Jesus said simply, "Pray the Lord of the harvest to send out laborers into His harvest" (Matt. 9:37-38). To Jesus, prayer was the key to the release of workers necessary to fulfill His Great Commission.

Reflecting on the challenging task of reaching all the world for Jesus, the great missionary statesman Andrew Murray came to this conclusion over a century ago:

> The man who mobilizes the Christian Church to pray will make the greatest contribution in history to world evangelization.[14]

Almost two decades ago I first met Jack McAlister, founder of Every Home for Christ (then called World Literature Crusade). I was impressed by an intense commitment for mobilizing systematic prayer, twenty-four hours a day. It would cover not only ministry activity in scores of nations but also passionate pleas for the opening of doors into all the nations of the world. I quickly learned that twenty-four-hour prayer was essential. Scripture tells us the "accuser of our brethren" functions in this capacity "day and night" (Rev. 12:10), and we must respond with a day-and-night counter-assault.

In conversing with Bill Bright, founder of Campus Crusade for Christ, I discovered that he, too, launched his ministry with a twenty-four-hour prayer chain that has continued unbroken for more than four decades. Could this be the primary reason such ministries have accomplished so much over the years?

Prayer obviously was at the heart of all significant advances made by the early church. In fact, the first recorded administrative decision the apostles made following the Day of Pentecost was that they would give themselves "continually to prayer and to the ministry of the word" (Acts 6:4). They had surveyed the remarkable growth of the church and determined they could no longer carry out all of the day-to-day demands brought on by the growth

(Acts 6:1-3). The apostles, therefore, appointed deacons to assist them.

Today, missionary and missiologist alike are recognizing the significance of the role of prayer in the harvest. C. Peter Wagner reported one specific example of how focused prayer impacted the harvest in Colombia. It was given to him by John Huffman of Christ for the Cities in Latin America. Huffman had told Wagner about an unusual harvest response that occurred in areas targeted with prayer.

According to Wagner:

> An Every Home Crusade was conducted in Medellin before and after the Christ for the Cities prayer teams prayed for certain neighborhoods. In those neighborhoods which did not have a prayer team, 10 percent of those who accepted the first Bible study lesson finished the series and signed the decision card. But in the neighborhoods which had a prayer team, 55 percent finished the course and signed the card....
>
> In the homes covered by prayer, eight out of ten accepted the first Bible Correspondence Course. This is one of the most significant case studies of the relationship between prayer and evangelism I have ever seen.[15]

Prayer's impact on the harvest globally is clearly evident. The miracle of the falling walls across the old Soviet Union and Eastern Europe should serve as special encouragement for those who are praying for similar miracles to take place in nations bound in darkness by such restrictive forces as Islam, Hinduism, Buddhism and numerous others. No obstacle can ultimately stand in the way of a praying church. And because there has never been a greater prayer movement in the history of the church than today, there is hope the world may indeed be evangelized in this generation — once and for all. ✄

TWELVE

HARVEST MIRACLES

*Catching a Glimpse of
the Lamb's Book of Life*

M Y WIFE and I were making our first trip to the South Pacific. We had come to survey the harvest miracles resulting from systematic island-to-island evangelism throughout Fiji's 106 inhabited islands.

Watching the young Fijian attach another sheet of names to the huge scroll, we noticed seven similar scrolls on the shelf behind him. We discovered that workers there had developed a unique way of recording the names of new converts.

From the outset of the campaign seven years earlier, someone had suggested preparing a scroll to list the name of each new believer. Now there were eight scrolls, each containing some four thousand individual names. So incredible was the growing harvest that it finally required a full-time worker just to process these new believers for follow-up as well as add their names to the expanding scrolls. On some days as many as two hundred names would be processed and recorded.

We soon learned the full scope of the harvest miracles of the Pacific. The scrolls were but a visual picture of the growing ingathering of souls taking place all over the world.

Unraveling one of the scrolls and examining scores of names reminded me of the Lamb's Book of Life that John spoke of in Christ's revelation to the apostle (see Rev. 20:12-15; 21:27). The unusual scroll also brought to my mind a letter that had crossed my desk almost a year earlier from a seventy-three-year-old Fijian grandmother. I wondered where her name appeared among the more than thirty thousand listed on the eight scrolls.

She lived on one of the distant islands of Fiji. Workers had traveled to her island, visiting every home and leaving a printed gospel message at each. When the EHC workers stopped at the grandmother's modest home, they had no idea how timely their visit was. They were greeted by the woman's grown children, who thanked the men for the printed message but indicated it was not a good time to talk. Their mother was very sick, and the island doctor didn't offer much hope for her recovery.

It was several weeks before these faithful workers returned to the main island and heard what happened to that simple seed they had planted on their journey. A letter from the elderly woman arrived at our EHC office in Fiji several days after her death. Later, a copy was sent to my desk as a testimony of praise. It read simply:

> I am 73 years of age and dying. The doctor says I will not live more than a few days. I have heard my children in the next room speak of my funeral. I am so thankful those two young men from Every Home Fiji came to our village three days ago. They visited our home and left a booklet with my children telling that Jesus Christ is the true Son of God. It said that by believing in Him we can have eternal life. Today, I have believed the message. I said a prayer to Jesus Christ just like the booklet suggested. Now my heart is at peace. I am no longer afraid to die.

A short time after she penned her letter, this elderly "newborn" saint went to be with Jesus. Her name was added to the Book of Life only hours before her death.

Miracle in the Surf

Occasionally these harvest miracles are the direct result of unusual signs and wonders that God uses to open the eyes of unbelievers. Such was the case when two young Fijian evangelists sailed courageously to a remote island in the Fijian chain where they had agreed to work with a young pastor to reach his island with the gospel.

Upon their arrival, which had been delayed by bad weather, the workers discovered that the pastor and his young wife had also been affected by the weather. It had been impossible to go fishing for several days. Since fish was their primary source of food, there would be no welcoming dinner. This was a deep embarrassment for the young pastor and his wife because strict island tradition called for a special meal to greet new visitors.

Fortunately, fasting wasn't an uncommon experience for these young Fijian evangelists who had been taught to fast and pray during their extensive training. They did, however, feel sad for the young pastor's wife who was obviously close to childbirth. They learned it was to be the couple's first. It was too bad, they thought, that she would have to go to bed hungry. What they didn't know was that the child would be born that very night.

Sometime past midnight, the young workers were awakened by the cries of a woman in childbirth. There would be no sleep that night. The evangelists prayed earnestly while the young pastor delivered the infant.

This was certainly a joyous occasion for the young couple. But the Christian workers now faced a dilemma like the one the pastor had faced the night before when there was no food to feed their visitors. Sending newly arrived guests to bed hungry was unthinkable in Fijian culture. But Fijians had another tradition, which was equally important. Whenever a couple gave birth to their first child, all friends and relatives, including those who might be visiting the couple, presented the mother and child with a special gift.

These workers were actually staying in the home of these new parents and lacked even a single Fijian dollar to purchase anything that might qualify as a gift. Theirs had been a journey of faith, and they arrived on the island penniless.

Dawn came early for the two evangelists. One of them, who had slept little, told his fellow worker he was going for a walk. He wanted to be alone to pray.

Wasn't God capable of supplying both the food for their stomachs as well as a blessing for this new child? he wondered as he walked along the sandy beach, praying. He, of course, knew the answer and promptly confessed his unbelief. Then, instinctively, he began praising God for His infinite ability to provide.

Suddenly, the worker's eyes glimpsed a bright-orange object bobbing in the surf not far from shore. It floated in just so close and then was carried back toward the vast expanse of ocean. The worker waded toward the object, which seemed to jerk suddenly at times, as a huge wave swept it ever closer.

Finally reaching the object, the young evangelist stared in disbelief. It was a brand new plastic baby washtub. He was sure it was new because the price tag was still attached — $12.95. No gift could possibly have been more appropriate for a new mother. But even more astounding were the contents of the floating tub, explaining its periodic jerking motion. Inside were two large fish, the most desirable species that could be found in those waters. Somehow they had become caught in the tub.

The excited evangelist rushed back to the village carrying not only a gift for the new mother and her infant, but two huge fish for the evening meal. Villagers soon heard of this amazing miracle that God had clearly used to open their hearts to the gospel. Within days many names from the island's main village and surrounding area were added to the Book of Life.

God's Heavenly Record

Sometimes the names of entire families are added to God's heavenly record beginning with just one member of a family who responds to the gospel. Sundar Das of eastern India is an example.

He had grown up in the predominantly Hindu district where the traditions and customs of the villagers were deeply rooted in the Hindu faith as well as tribal rituals. Most residents of the area were of the lower class of the Indian caste system. This system was supposedly outlawed years ago, but it still carries influence in certain areas of India.

For generations the Das family had been farmers by occupation. Like many villagers they had their own special guru from whom they might seek guidance on how to escape their impoverished condition. Through this season of their lives, idols were always present and served as objects of worship. Each family member even had his or her own personal idol.

Then one day in late summer villagers noticed two strangers approaching. They were visiting each home one by one, something the locals had not seen before. The curious eyes of the children followed every move of these two young visitors. What could they be carrying in the heavy bags strapped over their shoulders?

The visitors finally arrived at the Das home and struck up a conversation with the two oldest women of the clan. They gave them two gospel messages, one for children and the other for adults. The women were amazed to hear that the young men had walked forty miles from Calcutta, visiting every dwelling in each village along the way. Their journey had required many weeks of rigorous travel.

After the two evangelists were gone, Sundar Das began to read one of the messages — the message prepared specifically for adults. As he read it the first time, he felt a sharp stab in his heart. He read it again. The second time he was drawn to kneel in his darkened room as the sun was going down. The message actually didn't mention kneeling. It was something the young man simply felt led to do. He began to pray. In a moment his heart opened to the presence of Christ, and he knew something profound had happened. All he had ever known of the gospel was contained in the eight pages of the small pamphlet he had just read. Still, he knew he was a different person.

Sundar could not contain the joy of his newfound faith. No one told him that a Christian must also be a witness. He was just so full of joy that he immediately shared his new experience with everyone. But the ancestral beliefs of his family and the generations of idolatry seemed to hold his entire family in its grasp. Later he would receive all four lessons of EHC's Bible correspondence course. But for now the persistent witness of Sundar Das was based solely on the message of the eight-page gospel pamphlet and his life-changing personal encounter with Christ.

In a few days, the first burst of light came. Another family member responded positively to the gospel. Soon another responded, then another. Amazingly, in just three weeks all but one of the family members had received Christ as Savior. Only the elderly grandmother refused. She had been one of the first to receive the gospel messages from the strange visitors, but her lifelong beliefs in Hinduism had kept her bound in darkness. Still, all of her children and grandchildren had now been gloriously converted, and together they began praying for their grandmother.

Less than a month passed when the family awakened to discover that an amazing miracle had happened in the night. Sometime before dawn the grandmother had thrown away all of her idols. That morning she told her stunned family that she, too, had now accepted Christ as Savior.

That October the Christian workers returned to the village. In a small nearby pond they publicly baptized thirteen members of the Das family — something never before seen in their village. More than seventy Hindu villagers gazed inquisitively from the banks.

As they returned to their homes, the seventy observers swelled to more than a hundred. They seemed to sense that something profound had occurred. So strong was the impression left by the gathering that within a few weeks another public baptism was held in the same pond. This time an even greater number of villagers was baptized.

Today, if you were to visit this small town some forty miles from Calcutta, you would discover a thriving congregation of believers where scores of names have been added to the Lamb's Book of Life. And it all resulted from a single, anointed gospel message left at a farmer's hut in India more than a decade ago.

A Brother to My Paper

Some names added to the Lamb's Book of Life may never be known or recorded this side of heaven by missionaries or Christian workers. Years ago while traveling through the steaming jungles of East Africa, Austin Chawner, one of EHC's early African directors, stopped in a remote village. He did not know if a church had ever been planted in the region. Explaining what a Christian was, he asked the village chief if there were any such believers in his village.

"No," the chief replied. "But there is one man of the village who has been acting very strange for many months. He has quit drinking alcohol and no longer participates in our village dances." Eagerly the missionary asked if he might speak with the man.

The chief sent someone into the dense bush to locate the man while Chawner began giving out gospel booklets from hut to hut throughout the village. As he neared the end of the village's main road, a young man came running up to him, shouting, "That's a brother to my paper. You have a brother to my paper."

Out of his torn rags for clothing, the man pulled a well-worn piece of paper written in his native tongue. Chawner recognized it immediately. A year earlier he had gone through that part of Africa and had dropped that very gospel message on a road some distance from the village. This man had picked it up and read the message. With no other guidance than God's Spirit, he believed it to be true.

For almost a year he had maintained a Christian testimony in that village without having seen or heard of another black or white Christian. He did not even know there was such a thing as a missionary. Interestingly, had Austin Chawner never returned to that region in his lifetime, he still would have met this brother in heaven. His name had been recorded in the Book of Life.

A Serial Killer's Conversion

Some of the names added to the Lamb's heavenly record as the result of the printed page have included hardened criminals. Rajendra Jakkal, a serial killer from Pune, India, is one example.

The people of Pune and the entire police force had been both terrified and perplexed at a series of unprecedented murders and robberies that had rocked the city from November 1976 through April 1977. So great was the fear that the people dared not leave their homes after dusk. The streets were deserted. Houses were shut tight and doors chained. Taxi drivers were reluctant to go to the areas where the murders had occurred.

Within a few weeks of the first murders in November eighty-two police detectives had been pressed into service and were working day and night for a break in the case. Unfortunately, they lacked a single solid clue.

Then one morning the local newspaper carried the headline "The Murderers Are Arrested." It had been a lucky break for the police. Acting purely on suspicion, they had arrested two of the gang members for questioning. One of these, Rajendra Jakkal, age twenty-five, turned out to be the ringleader of the group. He had killed his own classmate, Prakash Hegde, the son of a hotel owner, when a ransom bid for his kidnapping failed. He threw the body into a nearby lake.

Police didn't know for certain if this crime was linked to the others until Rajendra's confession during the initial interrogation. Soon all six gang members were in custody. Their crimes were heralded as "crimes of the century" by many. One was particularly reminiscent of the horrible murders in California in August 1969, when numerous movie professionals were brutally murdered in a Beverly Hills mansion by a group called the Manson family.

The Pune gang had raided the house of Mr. Abhyankar, a leader in the civic government. He and his wife had just departed for a dinner engagement. Unfortunately, several others remained at home, including their youngest son, a brilliant medical student; their daughter, who worked as a receptionist at a nearby hotel; and their elderly parents. Also present was the family's household servant.

According to the police report, Rajendra Jakkal pressed the doorbell. When the door was opened slightly, the entire gang appeared and forced its way in. The next two hours became a living hell for the Abhyankar family and their servant. Each was brutally strangled before the gang departed with jewelry and cash.

Several days later, Rajendra and his gang murdered another young man named Anil. He also had been their schoolmate. Then, seven days later, on April 30, 1977, the entire gang was taken into custody.

The trial for the murders began in Pune in May 1978. It lasted for six months and concluded with the judge's sentencing four of the gang to be hanged, including Rajendra.

A full year later, in April 1979, the Bombay High Court confirmed the death sentence. The four convicts then appealed to the Indian Supreme Court, requesting their death sentences be commuted to life imprisonment. The appeal was dismissed in November 1980.

Their attorneys persisted in filing a review petition against the dismissal, but this also was rejected four months later in March 1981. Finally, in April 1982 the Indian Supreme Court directed that the four accused be hanged without further appeal. The executions were set for May 12, 1983, though they later were delayed until October 1983 for technical reasons.

But few of those who had watched the proceedings knew the amazing life-changing miracle that had begun several years earlier in the heart of one of the condemned murderers, Rajendra Jakkal.

The first sign of this miracle had begun on a cool November night in 1978 when the Every Home for Christ director at Pune was preparing to close his office and head for his nearby residence. The doorbell rang, and the director greeted one of his EHC field evangelists. He had come by the office late with an important prayer request. The local prison warden had granted EHC workers permission to visit Rajendra Jakkal the following day. The evangelist needed literature to give to the condemned man, and he requested special prayer. By now Jakkal had become a household name throughout much of India.

The evangelist and the director joined in a season of prayer, and the worker then departed with a set of EHC Bible lessons.

The next day several Christian workers seized this unusual opportunity to visit Rajendra Jakkal and give him Scripture lessons on what it meant to become a disciple of Jesus Christ. But many months passed following this initial encounter with no word coming from the convict. Then, three years and five months later in April 1982, EHC's follow-up department in Pune was amazed to receive a decision card from the convicted murderer. Accompanying his response were the answer sheets for all four lessons of EHC's standard four-part Bible correspondence course. Also included was a handwritten testimony describing the criminal's conversion.

Rajendra explained that while he was awaiting the decision of the Bombay High Court and the Indian Supreme Court, he had asked his friends to supply him with literature on Hinduism. Hinduism, after all, represented his religious roots.

Unsatisfied, Rajendra requested that his mother send him a copy of the Koran. Perhaps the teachings of Islam held answers to life's meaning. He read the Koran with a passion but still felt no peace. He then began to contemplate the gospel lessons that had been brought to his cell by Christian workers many months earlier. Rajendra soon realized that in no religious writings other than the Christian Bible was there a specific mention of the forgiveness of sins.

So, on a humid night in April 1982, five years after his arrest, Rajendra Jakkal, one of India's most notorious criminals, surrendered his life to Christ.

It was clear from the murderer's written testimony that a miracle had truly occurred. "Everybody in this world has sinned against God according to the Bible," he explained. "I am also a sinner. But through faith in the Lord Jesus Christ I have received salvation and the assurance of eternal life."

He added, "I am eager to know more about Christ. I have put my trust in Jesus Christ and have accepted Him as my Savior and Lord. I have a desire to take water baptism that I may openly confess Him as my Savior."

Rajendra clearly recognized his need to share his newfound faith with others. "It is my sincere prayer that others may also come to the saving knowledge of Jesus Christ and receive the gift of eternal life," he wrote. "I humbly dedicate myself to be a witness of His message of love and to strive to share the gospel with others."

During the many months leading up to Rajendra's execution, the EHC office in Pune sent the prisoner its monthly Christian devotional magazine. It shared testimonies of the work of EHC in India as well as important prayer requests. And it encouraged new converts to participate in the evangelization of their own people by adopting a small village and providing the modest finances (120 rupees, or just a few dollars) to reach every family in that village with a gospel message.

Rajendra read this challenge and wrote the EHC Pune office requesting information about adopting a village. Within days they sent the requested information. But no response came directly from the condemned believer.

Only later did our EHC director discover that the day before Rajendra was hanged he had written a final letter to his mother. In it he expressed his last request: "Mother, I want to adopt a village for gospel proclamation. This is my desire and last wish — that you should send 120 rupees on my behalf to the India Every Home Crusade."

Rajendra's mother honored his request, and a few days later the 120 rupees arrived.

On October 25, 1983, Rajendra Jakkal was led from his cell and hanged. The guard who took him to the gallows told his family and friends that his final words were from the Christian Bible:

Yea, though I walk through the valley of the shadow of death, I will fear no evil; for You are with me (Ps. 23:4).

It was yet another remarkable harvest miracle. Rajendra's name had indeed been added to the Lamb's Book of Life. ☒

THIRTEEN

WARFARE EVANGELISM

*Taking New Territory
Through Fasting and Prayer*

T HE CHALLENGE before the church to seize territory held in Satan's grasp for generations will require a strategy of both sacrifice and desperation. Ordinary strategies of evangelism without sufficient power will not succeed.

Certain demonic forces could not be cast out in Jesus' day apart from fasting and prayer (Matt. 17:21; Mark 9:29). The same will be true if we are to see the deliverance of entire nations so deeply entrenched in demonic enslavement. Warfare evangelism — that is, evangelism strategies initiated and sustained through aggressive seasons of fasting and prayer — will most certainly be essential.

A lesson from the Israeli scribe Ezra provides special insight into the role fasting and prayer plays in taking new territory. God's people had been held captive for seventy years under Babylonian rule. Now the time had come for the exiled Jews to return to Jerusalem. Interestingly, they were taking back what was once rightfully theirs. In the process of setting the nations free, we are only taking back that which is God's. Scripture tells us:

The earth is the Lord's, and all its fullness (Ps. 24:1).

As the Jews were about to embark on their historic return to Jerusalem, Ezra realized that potentially threatening enemies lingered along the way. They sought to rob God's people of their possessions along with the very promise of God through Abraham that they would bless all the nations of the world. So, before embarking on their journey, Ezra calls for a nationwide fast at the river Ahava.

Then I proclaimed a fast there at the river of Ahava, that we might humble ourselves before our God, to seek from Him the right way for us and our little ones and all our possessions (Ezra 8:21).

Ezra's call to a season of fasting and prayer included a threefold focus. First, they were to fast and pray that God would lead them in a "right way." This might be labelled the *guidance* focus of their fast. Quite simply, they sought God's direction.

For us to evangelize unreached peoples with the good news of Jesus, we need to know the "right way" of penetrating these dark regions. Enemies surely lurk along the way seeking to defeat us. Like the mountainous Kwaio peoples of the Solomon Islands who were evangelized only after days of fasting and prayer, the right way to penetrate the estimated sixty-five hundred remaining unreached people groups will most certainly involve strategies of fasting and prayer.

Second, Ezra summoned God's people to fast and pray on behalf of the protection of their "little ones." This could be described as the *assistance* focus of their fast. Ezra realized Israel needed God's assistance to complete their journey safely in order to protect a whole new generation of their people. The scribe knew that out of these "little ones" would come many future generations of God's people, but not if they were destroyed.

We, too, are seeking the salvation of entire generations of peoples by making possible their access to the gospel. Sadly, many generations of the mountainous Kwaio people (see chapter 4) never had access to the gospel until that small band of praying evangelists first broke the strongholds over their region through fasting and prayer.

Finally, Ezra called for God's people to fast and pray on behalf of their possessions. This was the *substance* focus of their fast. Ezra knew God cared about the resources His people would need in order to begin life anew when they returned to Jerusalem.

In our challenge to penetrate every unreached people group with the gospel, we desperately need God's wisdom in the wise use of our resources. Ezra didn't want to see God's people robbed of their substance while enroute to their promise. We, too, must contend, through fasting and prayer, for the proper allocation of resources necessary to see all the nations receive the good news of Jesus Christ. Quite possibly one of the greatest strongholds which limits the completion of the task of world evangelization in our generation is materialism in the body of Christ.

Especially noteworthy in this lesson from the life of Ezra is the reason the scribe felt stirred to call for their fast. Earlier he had boasted to King Artaxerxes that his God was fully capable of protecting them as they returned to Jerusalem. Apparently, the king had offered Ezra troops to help protect them on their journey, but Ezra declined boldly.

Then, as he finds himself leading God's people into enemy territory, he appears to have second thoughts.

> For I was ashamed to request of the king an escort of soldiers and horsemen to help us against the enemy on the road, because we had spoken to the king, saying, "The hand of our God is upon all those for good who seek Him, but His power and His wrath are against all those who forsake Him" (Ezra 8:22).

The record indicates that God responded to Ezra's call for fasting and prayer and faithfully led His people unharmed through enemy-infested territory. The Ezra lesson (when applied to what might be termed "warfare evangelism") is clear: *When you're about to seize new territory for Jesus, it's time to fast and pray.*

An Army of Annas

Fasting, although recognized as a vital aspect of spiritual breakthrough, is a difficult spiritual discipline to comprehend, let alone explain and apply. It is repeatedly referred to throughout Scripture as a sacrificial form of prayer that produces results available in no other way, as emphasized in the demoniac's deliverance when he was confronted by Christ (see Mark 9:14-29). Fasting, in scriptural terms, involves a sacrificial denial of necessary nourishment while one turns his or her attention to seeking after the ways of God as a part of that denial.

A fast may be as long as forty days, as we see in Moses' experience (Deut. 9:18-21); or it may be as brief as a portion of a day, as when David and his men "fasted until evening" because of the death of Saul and Jonathan (2 Sam. 1:11-12). In the New Testament we read the testimony of Cornelius, the centurion: "Four days ago I was fasting until this hour; and at the ninth hour [3:00 P.M.] I prayed in my house..." (see Acts 10:30). This would suggest that after eating a meal the previous evening, Cornelius did not eat again until sometime later that next afternoon or evening — a fast that lasted approximately twenty-four hours. Thus, to fast "until evening" is generally thought to mean fasting from the time one retires at night until the next evening's meal. This would mean sacrificing breakfast and lunch with the intention of devoting a portion of those times specifically to prayer.

It should also be noted that in both Old and New Testament passages, fasting was often a *corporate* spiritual activity, as was the case with the Ezra lesson cited earlier (see also Joel 1:13-14; Esth. 4:13-17; 2 Sam. 1:11-12; and Acts 13:1-3).

Fasting likewise can be a primary focus of a person's overall ministry. Such was the case of Anna, an eighty-four-year-old prophetess who gave her later years, day and night, to "fastings" and prayer (Luke 2:36-37). Perhaps the real secret to breaking the most formidable strongholds enslaving generations in such regions as the 10/40 Window will be an army of Annas. Age will not be the primary essential. Availability will.

The Esther Model

The urgent appeal for fasting and prayer in Esther's day is uniquely appropriate in defining warfare evangelism as it relates to penetrating unreached peoples with the gospel. In Esther's day, the future of an entire people group (the Jewish nation) was at stake. Through the evil plans of Haman (Esth. 3:1-6), the whole Jewish race was targeted for extinction.

Only God could spare His people. Esther and those close to her seemed to recognize that a miracle would not occur without a spiritual fight. From their understanding of the Scriptures, they knew fasting and prayer would be the key. Interestingly, long before any Jewish elders could have imagined the coming plot, God was setting in motion this miracle that only a call to fasting and prayer would someday release.

From the outset God ordained that Esther would take the place of Queen Vashti, the wife of King Ahasuerus (Esth. 2:1-17). Because Vashti had disobeyed an order from the king, a new queen had to be chosen. The entire nation was notified of this need.

Mordecai, a Jew who heard this appeal, thought immediately of his uncle's daughter, the beautiful young Esther who had been orphaned and was now in his care.

This was God's first step in laying the foundation for deliverance of the Jewish people. But that deliverance would not come without a subsequent spiritual fight involving a season of intensive fasting and prayer.

God further allowed a specific event to take place in Mordecai's life. It would be used later to bring the Jewish leader to the king's attention at a crucial point when God would intervene suddenly.

Of this event Scripture relates:

> In those days, while Mordecai sat within the king's gate, two of the king's eunuchs, Bigthan and Teresh, door-keepers, became furious and sought to lay hands on King Ahasuerus. So the matter became known to Mordecai, who told Queen Esther, and Esther informed the king in Mordecai's name (Esth. 2:21-22).

This action promptly led to the arrest of the two conspirators who were hanged for their treason. Scripture adds a vital footnote that later would be critical to the unfolding of God's plan:

> And it [the details of this matter] was written in the book of the chronicles in the presence of the king (Esth. 2:23).

Later, God used the vanity of evil Haman in bringing about the miracle. When King Ahasuerus promoted Haman to the highest seat of honor above all the princes (nobles) in Shushan, Haman expected all the servants within the palace gates to bow before him when he passed. Mordecai, being a devout Jew, refused, thus angering Haman (Esth. 3:1-5).

Mordecai's refusal to bow prompted Haman to begin a campaign to exterminate all the Jews throughout the vast province that stretched all the way from India to Ethiopia (Esth. 1:1). Consider the implications of this edict. Had Haman succeeded, there could have been no Messiah born from God's people as God had intended. Our salvation thus was at stake. Indeed, the future of all evangelistic efforts was being threatened. And that's where the power of a call to fasting and prayer enters the picture.

From this Esther model we glean four essential qualities of spirit, or prevailing attitudes, that help us understand the role of warfare evangelism in the salvation of a people group.

A Spirit of Desperation

Desperate saints taking desperate measures become God's finest warriors. Moses was desperate in crying out to God regarding the sins of Israel. He declared his willingness to have his name "blotted" from the record of the redeemed and was even ready to die, if necessary, for the desired deliverance (Ex. 32:32; Num. 11:14-15). Elijah was seized with a similar desperation as he fled the wrath of Jezebel (1 Kin. 19:4-8). Nehemiah, too, was first motivated to days of fasting and weeping over the conditions in Jerusalem. Then courage came to lead God's people to rebuild Jerusalem's fallen walls (Neh. 1-4).

Jesus, also, set the example. His desperation before going to the cross brought Him to such agony that His sweat became as blood (Luke 22:44).

We see the same desperation in both Mordecai and Esther (Esth. 4:1,16). When Mordecai realizes the king has actually approved a decree to destroy all of the Jews, he rips his clothing and cries out with a "loud and bitter cry." As the announcement goes forth, desperation spreads to every province, resulting in "great mourning among the Jews, with fasting, weeping, and wailing" (Esth. 4:3).

Fasting appears to be the natural outflow of their desperation. So it is today. Truly desperate believers sooner or later will feel the need to fast and pray. It comes with the territory. Indeed, *the territory comes with fasting!*

A Spirit of Consecration

The Esther model continues with a spirit of consecration. It might even be defined as *concentrated* consecration. It is fasting with a focus. Esther now pleads with Mordecai:

> Go, gather all the Jews who are present in Shushan, and fast for me...for three days...My maids and I will fast likewise (Esth. 4:16).

Now the fast was to become focused on Esther. Apparently the queen understood the power of concentrated, focused fasting. More than anyone else, she knew she was really going to need it.

Esther had, after all, already committed herself to go before King Ahasuerus and plead on behalf of the Jewish people. She appeared to have no idea exactly what to say but decided to trust God to give her wisdom.

Culturally, for a queen or any other subject to take such action in those days without the king's first summoning that person to his presence was tantamount to signing one's death sentence. The person's life, however, could be spared if the king stretched out his scepter toward that individual. Esther thus realized that in order to see favor in this tense circumstance, she would need God's intervention at the very moment she entered the king's chambers. A three-day fast was therefore consecrated among palace Jews and included the queen herself (Esth. 4:16).

A Spirit of Determination

Throughout this process a spirit of determination seemed to be growing in Queen Esther's heart. Mordecai had told her earlier:

> Who knows whether you have come to the kingdom for such a time as this? (Esth. 4:14).

By now Esther had determined that nothing would stop her from appealing to the king. She realized that if all the Jewish people were killed, she too would be included. She sent word to Mordecai to call for a three-day fast and said with quiet resignation:

> I will go to the king, which is against the law; and if I perish, I perish (Esth. 4:16b).

Esther's determination, saturated with the power of the three-day fast, did indeed release the favor she needed as she approached the king unannounced. Instantly, he held the scepter toward his queen (Esth. 5:2). Interestingly, Esther did not consider approaching the king until the third day of the concentrated fast.

When the king finally inquired as to the queen's desire, she simply requested a banquet with the king and Haman. The king, of course, had no idea what it was all about but promptly scheduled the banquet. He notified Haman, who was convinced some new honor was about to be bestowed on him and rushed home to inform his family.

Passing Mordecai in the courtyard, who yet refused to honor him, Haman was filled with indignation. When recounting to his wife, Zeresh, his good fortune of the banquet invitation, he complained of the one blemish on all his present fortune — Mordecai. Zeresh and his friends urged him to authorize the building of a gallows and, on the morning of the banquet, to suggest to the king that he order Mordecai hanged.

But that night another "divine coincidence" occurred. That it happened the very night the three-day fast concluded is not without significance. The king was unable to sleep and decided to have an aide read to him from the chronicles of the kings (Esth. 6:1). As dawn approached, the king was read the specific account of Mordecai's saving his life, perhaps years earlier, when two of the king's officers had sought to assassinate him (Esth. 2:21-23). Only then did the king ask whether the one who spared his life had ever received proper recognition for this act. "Nothing has been done for him," the aide responded (Esth. 6:3).

By then it was early morning. The king asked the aide if anyone had entered the court yet. At that precise moment, Haman entered, hoping to gain approval for the execution of Mordecai. It appeared he was about to get his opportunity when the king summoned him to his throne. However, before Haman could express his wishes, the king himself asked a question:

> What shall be done for the man whom the king delights to honor? (Esth. 6:6).

Vanity again filled Haman's heart because he was convinced the king was speaking of him.

Haman suggested:

> For the man whom the king delights to honor, let a royal robe be brought which the king has worn, and a horse on which the king has ridden...Then let this robe and horse be delivered to the hand of one of the king's most noble princes, that he may array the man whom the king delights to honor. Then parade him on horseback through the city square (Esth. 6:7-9).

To Haman's utter astonishment, the king responded:

> Hurry, take the robe and the horse, as you have suggested, and do so for Mordecai the Jew (Esth. 6:10).

In humiliation Haman obeyed, fearing, with good reason, what might happen if Mordecai was elevated to a position of power above his.

Later, in Haman's presence at the banquet, Esther revealed his evil plans to the king, who became so enraged he rushed into the palace garden (Esth. 7:7). Returning, he found Haman lying upon

Esther's bed, beside her, pleading for his life. Angrily the king declared:

> Will he even molest the queen while she is with me in the house? (Esth. 7:8, NIV).

A nearby aide promptly informed the king that Haman had earlier built a gallows intending to hang Mordecai. The king responded immediately, "Hang him on it!" (Esth. 7:9). Thus, the weapon that the enemy had formed for his own evil intent was turned against him, all of which resulted from fasting and prayer.

A Spirit of Jubilation

What was born out of an almost hopeless sense of desperation and sustained with qualities of a selfless consecration and determination erupted into a sweeping spirit of jubilation. The Esther model for warfare evangelism concluded with this observation:

> So Mordecai went out from the presence of the king in royal apparel of blue and white, with a great crown of gold and a garment of fine linen and purple; and the city of Shushan rejoiced and was glad. The Jews had light and gladness, joy and honor. And in every province and city, wherever the king's command and decree came, the Jews had joy and gladness (Esth. 8:15-17).

Today, our heavenly King's command and decree focus on the liberating message of the gospel. It has already been issued from the King Himself but must be taken to "every province and city" throughout the earth. When that happens, "light and gladness, joy and honor" will fill the earth. Ordinary evangelism (if there is such a thing) may work in ordinary places (if there are such locations), but certain strongholds most surely will require something more. Warfare evangelism could well be the key. It is certainly worth a try. ⧗

FOURTEEN

WARFARE INTIMACY

The Joshua Posture for
Possessing God's Promises

I T WAS an unusual impression that flooded my heart. I was certain the Lord was talking to me, but this time He wasn't giving me a direct command but rather asking a question: "Have you ever considered spending an entire month in simply ministering unto Me?"

Moments earlier I had received a clear directive from the Lord. I was to confront the strongholds of communism in Eastern Europe through prayer, beginning with a trip to Berlin. This would ultimately result in my journeying to the Berlin Wall to pray the five-word prayer described in chapter 1. The night of this visitation I had been ready to head to the airport. But I knew I wasn't prepared. Something had to happen first. And it wouldn't be easy.

"Have you ever considered spending an entire month in simply ministering unto Me?" The words filled my mind again. Could God be serious? At least I felt consoled in that He appeared to be asking and not insisting. Perhaps I should just answer, "Not really," and maybe the impression would go away, I thought.

But tears began flowing as I realized it was too late for that. In having heard the question, I knew that only a positive response would lead me to God's best for my future ministry. Like Joshua, who encountered the Commander-in-chief of heaven's army before the Jericho miracle (Josh. 5:13-15), I too needed a special encounter with my Captain. But only later did I realize this encounter would continue for an entire month.

Restoration and Rejoicing

How does one go about spending a month "ministering unto the Lord"? I understood what it meant to spend a day in prayer, because our ministry had conducted a monthly day of prayer for almost ten years. These were days I spent in prayer with area intercessors and staff. At the outset we called them days of R and R, or days set aside for "restoration and rejoicing." Each day was an occasion for me to retreat from ministry cares into a spiritual rest in Jesus while rejoicing in His goodness.

But even these days were sometimes tiring. Prayer can be work, especially if it continues for an entire day. So it's easy to understand one's anxiety when contemplating a complete month devoted to seeking God in prayer.

I remembered reading of how "Praying Hyde," the Presbyterian missionary to India, once spent thirty days in continuous prayer. But that was a different generation, I thought. And, besides, I reasoned, Praying Hyde was simply "made" that way.

Still other questions flooded my mind. How does a leader explain to his staff that he's not making any appointments or taking any calls — for a month? And if much of that ministry's income is derived from their leader's seminars and other speaking engagements, as was my case, how would we make ends meet?

All this flooded my mind as I contemplated a month given to waiting on God in prayer. I sensed God was calling me to a new level of intimacy with Him. Without it the best of His future blessings might never be realized. And just as a child cannot be conceived without the intimacy of marital union, I knew some blessings God desired to birth in me first had to be conceived in prayer.

It was only a few days before December 1987, as I faced these questions during that same midnight prayer encounter that would later result in my going to the Berlin Wall. But first, I decided, it would be necessary to say yes to this unusual heart impression and, whatever it meant, spend that month in prayer.

During the next three days a plan unfolded as to how this month of prayer would be conducted. Some days I was to invite other intercessors to join me. Other days would be spent alone. Most days would consist of waiting quietly on the Lord, a discipline I had never really attempted for a whole day.

As I mapped out the month's prayer schedule, I realized God was not suggesting I pray sixteen to eighteen hours a day, but rather that I set aside my normal office hours just to seek His presence.

I also felt impressed to spend several of the days concentrating on rather specific acts of prayer and worship. For example, I had never spent a prolonged season in prayer literally on my face, especially for an entire day. Nor had I ever spent a full day thanking God for all those people who had blessed Dee and me with their financial support. Both of these activities were to be combined in a day spent prostrate before God thanking Him "by name" for every person who had made our ministry possible. It was also to be a day of almost continuous tears as I prayed through hundreds of names, one by one, thanking God for their faithfulness.

Heart Songs

But most memorable of the month's focuses was to be an entire day of simply singing "heart songs" to the Lord in prayer (Eph. 5:19; Col. 3:16).

Singing a song unto the Lord in prayer certainly wasn't an uncommon personal experience. In *The Hour That Changes the World*,[1] one of my earliest books on how to develop a practical plan for daily prayer, I devoted an entire chapter to singing songs of worship during prayer. In my research for the book I had discovered that many saints of the past had sung spontaneously composed "heart songs" in prayer. Some at times had actually sung their prayers. Perhaps this is what the psalmist meant by his reference to singing a "new song" as a part of his worship (Ps. 144:9).

Years ago, upon realizing the psalms were originally written as spiritual songs, I began singing through them systematically, a few each week, making up my own melodies for each psalm. (The longer psalms, such as 78, 106 and 119, I divided up over several days.)

But never had I thought of spending an entire day simply ministering unto the Lord singing "spiritual songs." I realized, of course, that I wouldn't be singing constantly and that there might be some moments of quiet waiting during my worship. But still the thought of spending such a day was intriguing. Little could I have known this would be a day that would change my life forever.

I invited several of our staff as well as regular intercessors to join me for a portion of the day, primarily because I thought I might need some help. I also knew that some, such as I, probably wondered what it would be like to spend a prolonged season exclusively in song. It was, to say the least, a most unusual day.

A Song of Conception

By mid afternoon my voice was weary, though a strange joy was growing inside me.

Then one of our senior staff began to sing his own heart song, providing me with a moment of rest. He sang a made-up song that I initially thought was a little silly. "Lord," he intoned, "our culture has a saying, 'We make our bed and therefore must lie in it....' "

I wondered where he might be going with this strange song. He continued, "But, Lord, we have chosen to make for You a bed of song, and we come with our melodies just to love You!"

What happened next is almost impossible to describe. When the staff member finished, I picked up his theme and continued singing a song of love for the Lord. I expressed how much I longed to be close to Him, to touch Him, to know Him. Suddenly the room seemed to be filled with the fullness of His presence.

If it's possible to sing a song consisting only of tears, that is what happened next. I seemed caught up, literally, in a heavenly embrace. I had just sung that I wanted to touch God and hold Him, but in reality He had touched me. Now *He* was holding me. So deep was the sense of intimacy that I lost all awareness of time.

To describe the experience as divine romance hardly seems adequate in portraying the passion of the moment. The danger of using such expressions in referring to spiritual matters is that we tend to think of romance and passion strictly in terms of human sexuality. But this was light years beyond such comparisons. I wanted more of God — period. And He was there.

What time I left the prayer room at our office, I cannot remember. I do recall my arrival at home that evening. I wanted to spend a few more quiet moments in my backyard prayer chapel at home, reflecting on the uniqueness of the day and recording my impressions in my prayer diary.

How can one adequately describe such moments of supernatural romance? It seemed as if something of a divine conception had taken place. When a man and woman come together in the intimacy of marriage, I reasoned, there is always the possibility for conception. Could something similar, but on a spiritual level, take place in our intimate moments with Jesus? Could it be that some of our prayers actually conceive what later will be birthed as we wait patiently for God's timing?

My eyes caught a glimpse of the new 1988 calendar I had just purchased and tacked to my prayer-room bulletin board. It was the middle of December 1987. A thought suddenly filled my mind: It will be born sometime in 1988!

What will be born? I wondered. And how long will it take? I thought of a baby in the mother's womb maturing from a fertilized speck of life. Nine months later it would emerge from the womb to express its fullness in life.

God's timing in the process of birthing His blessings certainly doesn't always match human time tables. But my heart immediately felt assured that something new and exciting would be born into my experience in exactly nine months.

What it might involve, I could not say. I did sense it would somehow focus on the unfinished task of world evangelization.

I removed the tacks holding the small calendar to the bulletin board and began counting the days, month by month. I stopped at September 12, exactly nine months later. I wrote: "Something new will be born today!"

Berlin and Beyond

The new year began with my memorable trip to the Berlin Wall where I spoke the five-word prayer "In Jesus' name, come down!" just days after my month in prayer concluded.

The following summer we took the team of youthful intercessors to Eastern Europe, including Bulgaria and Romania. There our Jericho prayer walk around Romania's communist headquarters in Bucharest took place where those miracle seeds of prayer were planted in the large central park in Sofia, Bulgaria (see chapter 1).

All this occurred while I served as executive director of a small prayer ministry we had founded in 1982 called Change the World Ministries. But little did I realize this leadership role was about to change, and the month of intimacy with God was the key factor. In our prayer ministry we had mobilized many thousands of hours of prayer for the evangelization of a lost world. Now it appeared we would soon become much more directly involved in the answer to those prayers.

The summer trip to Eastern Europe with our band of young prayer warriors was about to begin. Just days earlier, Andy Duda, chairman of the board of directors for Every Home for Christ had contacted me on behalf of their executive committee with a challenging proposal: Would I consider merging Change the World Ministries and its prayer focus with Every Home for Christ's house-to-house literature evangelism strategy? In this merger I would become their international president. If I consented to allow my name to be submitted, I was told, the full board would have to approve. That process would probably not be completed until sometime in late August or early September.

Little could I have known, as our prayer team traveled from town to town across Bulgaria and Romania, praying for the evangelization of every family in every village, that our prayers, particularly for me, would soon be answered in a most practical manner. Even as we were praying through these villages, the board of directors of Every Home for Christ was meeting six thousand miles away regarding the merging of our ministries.

171

Nor could I have known that just fifteen months later the Berlin Wall would come crashing down, and dictators of such countries as Bulgaria and Romania would be banished forever from power. This would make possible the very systematic, house-to-house evangelism we had prayed for during this initial prayer journey. I didn't know it at the time, but a year later I would be planning the systematic house-to-house evangelization of places like Berlin — and beyond — as the new international president of Every Home for Christ.

By the first week in September 1988, the full board of Every Home for Christ made its final decision for a total merger of the two ministries. I was invited to serve as their new international president. But in spite of almost three months of indications that this might occur, it was now happening with unusual speed. I wondered if there might be a more reasonable time span to facilitate this coming together. But the board of Every Home for Christ suggested the merging be completed as quickly as possible since the ministry had been without a president for almost a year.

"When do you think I should begin my new role?" I asked board chairman Andy Duda.

"Could you possibly begin a week from Monday?" he responded.

I was on a ministry trip to Arizona when we spoke by phone. A week from Monday seemed unusually sudden.

"Let's see," I said, as I fumbled through my wallet looking for a small pocket calendar. "That would be...*September 12.*"

I'm sure Andy could not have understood the significance of my momentary pause as I stared at the date. In my mind I could picture another calendar clearly, at home in my backyard prayer chapel. I recalled the notation I had made nine months earlier with a felt-tipped pen on day number 12 for September, acknowledging that this would be a day of birthing that actually began in those hours of intimacy the previous December.

Several days later I was back in California to begin my first day as international president of Every Home for Christ. I would be overseeing seventy global offices and ten thousand staff and volunteers who weekly would visit 350,000 new homes where the gospel would be planted. Many thousands of these homes would be in Bulgaria and Romania where we had prayed earlier that summer.

That night, as I went into my prayer room, I gazed at the small calendar attached to the bulletin board. It was September 12. I wiped tears from my eyes as I read six simple words: *"Something new will be born today."*

Warfare Intimacy

At first glance, the term *warfare* hardly seems to fit alongside the word *intimacy*. Yet I have chosen to title this final chapter "Warfare Intimacy" because I'm convinced that intimacy with the Lord is the primary essential to all victorious warfare. For me, I will certainly never doubt that the intimacy I experienced with the Lord in prayer in mid-December 1987 had something profound to do with the new door of opportunity that opened exactly nine months later on September 12, 1988.

When Joshua looked toward the towering Canaanite fortress of Jericho, he was looking at a problem. But suddenly he saw the *Solution!* It wasn't a strategy or a concept. It wasn't a plan but a *Person.* Enter the Captain! Before him stood the "Commander of the army of the Lord" (Josh. 5:14). There is no mention in the text that Joshua ever looked again toward the problem. He was consumed with the *Solution!*

Joshua knew he was in the presence of the Lord. This was, as mentioned earlier in chapter 6, what theologians call a *christophany,* a pre-incarnate appearance of Christ Himself. The act of worship and humility that followed this encounter with the Captain might well be described as "warfare intimacy."

The Lord didn't actually command Joshua to fall on his face and worship Him. The Israeli leader simply did it instinctively. Neither did Joshua ask his Captain specifically for a strategic plan to help him conquer Jericho. He was simply caught up in Jesus. In reverence and awe, flat on his face, he pleaded:

What message does my Lord have for his servant? (Josh. 5:14, NIV).

Notice that the Lord didn't respond by saying, "I've come with a plan to help you capture Jericho!" Instead He commanded Joshua:

Take off your sandals, for the place where you are standing is holy (Josh. 5:15, NIV).

True, in the next chapter a clear strategy was indeed given to
Joshua. But there's no record he had risen yet from his prostrate
position to receive it. How long he was on his face we do not
know. We do know this: Joshua's warfare intimacy was a definite
key to Israel's ultimate victory.

Wisdom for Our Warfare

Although warfare prayer is most often associated with a kind of
fervent intensity, one must not overlook the role spiritual intimacy
plays in the birthing of our personal victories. In the case of
Joshua, it was only as he humbled himself in worship before the
Lord that specific directions came for a truly strategic victory.
Intimacy with our Lord must therefore be viewed as essential to
our receiving divine direction necessary for future warfare victories.

One of Scripture's most basic lessons on receiving such direction is Proverbs 3:5-6. It was one of the first Bible passages I recall
memorizing as a youth:

Trust in the Lord with all your heart, and lean not on
your own understanding; in all your ways acknowledge
Him, and He shall direct your paths.

Hidden in this passage is one of Scripture's truly great lessons
on the role of spiritual intimacy in receiving God's guidance for
victory-assured warfare.

We are first admonished to "trust in the Lord" with *all* our hearts.
This speaks of implicit surrender. Trust means that we allow someone to act on our behalf without being afraid or having misgivings.

We are next cautioned to guard against personal opinions that
may bend us toward human reasoning in the decision-making
process. "Lean not on your own understanding," we're advised.
Finally, we are instructed to "acknowledge" the Lord uncondition-
ally in all our "ways."

Two words in this passage are especially significant in this

174

matter of warfare intimacy: *ways* and *acknowledge*. "In all your ways," we are told, "acknowledge Him."

The word *ways* is derived from the Hebrew expression *derek*, meaning "a road, a course (such as a course of life), or a mode of action." This pictures a path or course that affords passage from one place to another. *Derek* also refers to a way of life, or the essence of one's lifestyle. It can include very specific opportunities a person may encounter on a recurring basis. Thus, this passage may well be suggesting "in all your *opportunities, acknowledge* God."

Of course, one of the most recurring segments of opportunity experienced by believers on a regular basis is the dawning of each new day. Every day is filled with fresh opportunities. It is almost as if this passage is suggesting, "In all your *days* acknowledge God." The thought is that if we'll just acknowledge God daily, applying all that this word *acknowledge* means, we are guaranteed wisdom for our ongoing warfare. The promise concludes: "He will direct your paths," or, as the NIV translates the phrase, "make your paths straight."

The Yada Factor

But here we discover the real secret to this entire lesson. It is found in the Hebrew word for "acknowledge" — *yada*. Elsewhere in the Old Testament *yada* is most frequently translated "know."

Generally, *yada* refers to someone possessing knowledge of another individual, place or circumstance. It is to know a person or thing. The word, however, employs a variety of definitions that, when taken as a whole, significantly enhances its contextual use in Proverbs 3:6. *Yada*, for example, also means to know someone by observation, investigation, reflection and firsthand experience. At times *yada* represents an even higher level of knowing — knowledge that is gained only from direct intimate contact. In fact, *yada* at this level speaks more of heart intimacy than it does of head knowledge.

The words *intimate* and *contact* are essential to our understanding of what the writer may well have had in mind when he penned Proverbs 3:5-6. Could he have been speaking of touching God intimately rather than just acknowledging the Creator's existence?

175

Later, Daniel employed the same expression, *yada,* when he declared, "The people who know their God shall be strong, and carry out great exploits" (Dan. 11:32). Note the qualities Daniel discussed that accompany those who truly know God. The word *strong* means "firm and durable." *Exploits* means "bold deeds and daring acts." But all of this is predicated on knowing God.

In using this word, *yada,* translated here as simply "know," Daniel obviously was referring to much more than a casual knowledge of God. In a New Testament sense, Daniel was even going beyond the new birth experience in using the term *yada.* This is not to suggest that some are more "saved" than others, but it is to suggest that some believers have more power than others. Christians may be born again but never rise to accomplish "bold deeds" or "daring acts" as the result of their Christian commitment or walk.

Perhaps when Daniel, as well as the author of the third chapter of Proverbs, used the word *yada* in their messages, they had in mind one of the earliest usages of the term *yada* in Hebrew culture.

The Genesis record provides an example: "Now Adam *knew* Eve his wife, and she conceived" (Gen. 4:1, italics added). Here the word *yada,* translated "knew," is referring to sexual intimacy that leads to conception. The NIV translates this passage, "Adam lay with his wife Eve, and she conceived." "Lay" here may have been deemed appropriate by the translators, but it is weak in its totality of meaning. A better translation may have been "Adam held his wife Eve intimately, and she conceived." *Yada* in this sense pictures the closest intimacy possible in the human relationship.

Looking again at the Daniel passage, the use of the word *yada* suggests that only those who touch God intimately will ever truly accomplish bold deeds and daring acts (Dan. 11:32).

The use of the expression *yada* in our Proverbs passage, then, becomes especially significant. It suggests that, after we've fully submitted to God in total trust, and we've firmly rejected our own human ways of reasoning, the final key to receiving absolute guidance in all our ongoing warfare is to maintain daily, intimate contact with the Lord. "In all your ways acknowledge Him" clearly suggests, "In all your opportunities, touch God intimately." Simply stated, *yada* with God (that is, intimate contact with Him) is the key factor in all victorious warfare.

Warfare Passion

Warfare prayer in most recent definitions would seem to suggest a bold, authoritative assault against definable enemy entities. But we must not overlook the fact that many of the great victories in ancient scriptural battles resulted simply from the welcoming of God's presence onto the battlefield (see Ex. 14:13; 2 Chr. 20:17). God's glory, in and by itself, is certainly capable of driving multitudes of demons fleeing in every direction.

What, then, is the key to victorious warfare and the possessing of God's promises? The answer, quite simply, is a passion for God's presence. Moses declared, "If Your presence does not go with us, don't let us go up from here" (Ex. 33:15, author's paraphrase).

Note also the example of ancient Israel regarding their seventy-year Babylonian captivity. Promising their eventual release, God declared:

> After seventy years are completed at Babylon, I will visit you and perform My good word toward you, and cause you to return to this place [Jerusalem] (Jer. 29:10).

The promise continues:

> For I know the thoughts that I think toward you, says the Lord, thoughts of peace and not of evil, to give you a future and a hope (Jer. 29:11).

But here we discover a linkage between this hope-filled promise for the future and the willingness of God's people to seek Him. Intimacy is related to victory. God adds:

> Then you will call upon Me and go and pray to Me, and I will listen to you. And you will seek Me and find Me, when you search for Me with all your heart (Jer. 29:12-13).

God had promised Israel that after seventy years of Babylonian captivity, He would honor His promised word to them and bring them back to their homeland. It was, however, a promise contingent on Israel's willingness to rely fully on Him. He alone would be their victory. Thus, they had to "search" for Him with "all" their hearts (Jer. 29:13).

Implied in such passages as this Jeremiah account is a quest for God that includes a level of intensity in our intimacy well beyond what might be termed "ordinary" prayer. The very word *search,* accompanied by the phrase "with all your heart," suggests an earnestness that borders on desperation. Derived from the Hebrew word *darash, search* suggests a following after or close pursuit of that which is desired. It further implies a passionate diligence in the searching process. It is like a lover diligently and passionately pursuing the object of his love.

In 2 Chronicles 15:2 where the prophet Azariah promises that the Lord will be with His people if they seek after Him, *darash* is the Hebrew word employed. Again, we see an implied emphasis on passion, intensity and diligence.

Darash is likewise used in 2 Chronicles 11:16 to describe the Levites who "set their heart to seek the Lord." Note the implied intensity and passion of one who sets his heart to seek after God. Such intensity suggests a passionate pursuit of the Lord Himself, not merely a seeking after His blessings or even the desire for victory in one's warfare. It is a quest not so much to get answers but to touch God!

The relationship between seeking God and experiencing victory in battle is also seen in such passages as 2 Chronicles 34:1-4. King Josiah, at only sixteen years of age, begins to "seek (*darash*) the God of his father David" which results in the total purge of Judah and Jerusalem of all the high places and demonic images in just four years. And this deliverance is clearly the result of Josiah's warfare intimacy which the Bible tells us begins "while he was still young."

Interestingly, King Uzziah also was but sixteen years of age when he began his reign. He, too, was pictured as one who sought God while still young (2 Chr. 26:1,5). This passion for God resulted not only in his prosperity (v. 5), but also in his later successes in warfare against enemy strongholds throughout Israel (see 2 Chr. 26:5-15). In each of these cases, God's people did not seek after victory as such, but rather after God Himself. They recognized that His presence alone meant victory.

Could there be a vital lesson in these ancient biblical models for warring believers today? I believe there is. We must first touch God before we can transform a troubled world. Intimacy with God, then, could well be the key to what theologians and missiologists refer to as closure regarding eventual fulfillment of the Great Commission. It's the *yada* factor in the overall equation to evangelize the world in our generation. Those closest to God in the conflict will hear Him far more distinctly than those lingering in the distance.

As A. W. Tozer, in his classic work *The Pursuit of God,* reminds us:

> The great of the Kingdom have been those who loved God more than others did.[2]

The gifted scholar further suggests that a careful look at past Bible characters and even well-known Christian leaders since New Testament times reveals each was vastly different from the others. There were differences in race, nationality, education, temperament and personal qualities. Yet, in one vital quality, they were clearly alike. Tozer explains:

> I venture to suggest that the one vital quality which they had in common was spiritual receptivity. Something in them was open to heaven, something which urged them Godward. Without attempting anything like a profound analysis, I shall say simply that they had spiritual awareness and that they went on to cultivate it until it became the biggest thing in their lives. They differed from the average person in that when they felt the inward longing they *did something about it.* They acquired the lifelong habit of spiritual response. They were not disobedient to the heavenly vision. As David put it neatly, "When thou saidst, Seek ye my face; my heart said unto thee, Thy face, Lord, will I seek" (Ps. 27:8).[3]

Seeking God's face is at the heart of all lasting spiritual success. We need God in our strategies, whether the goal is to raise our children, strengthen our marriages, succeed on the job, revive our churches or evangelize the world. The warfare in all of these endeavors is certain to increase.

But one thing is clear — those nearest to God in the battle stand the least likelihood of suffering defeat. A. W. Tozer sums it up well:

> When religion has said its last word, there is little we need other than God Himself.[4]

Perhaps that's why the psalmist, in describing his warfare and the need to stay close to the Lord in the battle, declared, "But as for me, I get as close to him as I can" (Ps. 73:28, TLB). ⌛

Introduction

1. David Bryant, from a paper titled *Reflections on Spiritual Warfare and the Ministry of United Prayer,* Concerts of Prayer International, P.O. Box 36008, Minneapolis, MN 55435.

2. Edgardo Silvoso, from a message given at the U.S. AD 2000 and Beyond Movement's preconsultation on citywide evangelism, Phoenix, Arizona, 1 September 1992.

Chapter 1: The Jericho Hour

1. George Otis Jr., from a taped message titled "Understanding the Times," given in Colorado Springs, Colorado, April 11, 1992. See also *The Last of the Giants* (Grand Rapids, Mich.: Chosen Books, 1991), pp. 144-146.

2. Otis, *The Last of the Giants,* p. 144.

3. Ibid.

4. Richard Rodriguez, "Latin Americans Convert from Catholicism to a More Private Protestant Belief," *Los Angeles Times,* 13 August 1989, Opinion section, p. 1.

Chapter 2: Praying Back the King

1. Walter Wink, "History Belongs to the Intercessors," *Sojourners,* October 1990.

2. Graham Kendrick and Chris Robinson, *All Heaven Waits,* Copyright © 1986, Thank You Music, P. O. Box 75, Eastbourne, BN23 GNW, United Kingdom.

Chapter 3: Divine Coincidences

1. For information on Every Home for Christ's Change the World School of Prayer home study course or church video program, write: Every Home for Christ, P. O. Box 35950, Colorado Springs, CO 80935-3595.

Chapter 4: Warfare Realities

1. *Los Angeles Times,* 11 November 1984, p. 3.

2. "Government Brings Famine to Ethiopia," *Los Angeles Times,* 11 November 1984, Opinion section, p. 1.

3. "Has Eritrea, Where Africa's Famine Began, Been Forgotten?," *Los Angeles*

Times, 19 October 1986, Calendar section, p. 3.

4. "The Teeth of Wind," *Time* magazine, 18 August 1986, p. 13.

5. Doug Struck, "Death Watch Over Sudan," *The Denver Post,* 9 May 1993, p. 10A.

6. Ibid.

7. From the testimony of Ralph Mahoney, World Missionary Assistance Plan, 900 N. Glenoaks, Burbank, CA 91502.

8. C. Peter Wagner, ed., *Engaging the Enemy* (Ventura, Calif.: Regal Books, 1991).

9. George Otis Jr., *Breaking the Strongholds in Your City,* edited by C. Peter Wagner (Ventura, Calif.: Regal Books, 1993), pp. 33-34.

Chapter 5: Penetrating the Darkness

1. Paul E. Billheimer, *Destined for the Throne,* (Fort Washington, Pa.: Christian Literature Crusade, 1975), p. 17.

2. Reinhard Bonnke, from a message given at Westminster Central Hall, London, England, 11 June 1993, at which the author participated.

Chapter 6: A View Toward Jericho

1. Abraham Lincoln, quoted in Dick Eastman and Jack Hayford, *Living and Praying in Jesus' Name* (Wheaton, Ill.: Tyndale House, 1988), p. 181.

2. Victor H. Matthews, *Manners and Customs of Bible Lands,* (Peabody, Mass.: Hendrickson, 1991), p. 250.

Chapter 7: Extraordinary Prayer

1. For information on forming a small strategic prayer group called a Jericho Chapter, write: Every Home for Christ, P. O. Box 35950, Colorado Springs, CO 80935-3595.

2. C. Peter Wagner, *Warfare Prayer* (Ventura, Calif.: Regal Books, 1992), p. 2.

3. Ibid., p. 4.

4. Edgardo Silvoso, from a message given at the U.S. AD 2000 and Beyond Movement's preconsultation on citywide evangelism, Phoenix, Arizona, 1 September 1992.

Chapter 8: Strategic-Level Prayer

1. Wesley Duewel, quoted in *Kneeling We Triumph*, compiled by Edwin and Lillian Harvey (Chicago: Moody Press, 1974), p. 44.

2. O. Hallesby, *Prayer* (Minneapolis: Augsburg Publishing House, 1959), pp. 130-131.

3. S. D. Gordon, *Quiet Talks on Prayer* (Pyramid Publications, 1967), p. 27.

4. *The Spirit Filled Life Bible,* New King James Version, edited by Jack Hayford, Litt.D. (Nashville: Thomas Nelson Publishers, 1991), p. 1424.

5. *Merriam Webster's Collegiate Dictionary*, Tenth Edition.

Chapter 10: A Promise to Moscow

1. Cindy Jacobs, *Possessing the Gates of the Enemy* (Grand Rapids, Mich.: Chosen Books, 1991), pp. 146-147.

2. C. Peter Wagner, *Your Spiritual Gifts Can Help Your Church Grow* (Glendale, Calif.: Regal Books, 1979), p. 228.

3. Jacobs, *Possessing the Gates of the Enemy*, p. 151.

4. *The Spirit Filled Life Bible*, p. 1988.

Chapter 11: Once and for All

1. Patrick Johnstone, *Operation World* (Bromley, Kent, England: STL Books, 1986 edition), p. 467.

2. John Hash, editor, *The Bible Pathway Story* (Murfreesboro, Tenn.: Bible Pathway Ministries), p. 9.

3. *The 25th Hour in Southeast Asia* (Studio City, Calif.: World Literature Crusade, 1971), p. 66.

4. Bob Hoskins, *All They Want Is the Truth* (Miami: Life Publishers, 1985), pp. 43-44.

5. Ibid., p. 90.

6. A. Clark Scanlon, from a paper titled *Global Survey of the Unfinished Task*, Foreign Mission Board, Southern Baptist Convention, presented to the Consultation on Global Survey of the Unfinished Task, Colorado Springs, Colorado, 20 July 1993.

7. From *God's Word and Literature Track: Goals and Objectives*, available from Every Home for Christ, P. O. Box 35950, Colorado Springs, CO 80935-3595.

8. From the registry of unreached peoples compiled by Frank Kaleb Jansen, Adopt-a-People Clearing House, Colorado Springs, Colorado.

9. From a concluding message given at Adopt-a-People Consultation II in Colorado Springs, Colorado, 25-26 April 1993.

10. Luis Bush, *AD 2000 and Beyond — A Handbook* (Colorado Springs, Colo.: AD 2000 and Beyond Movement), p. 11.

11. S. D. Gordon, *What Will It Take to Change the World?* (Grand Rapids, Mich.: Baker Book House, reprinted 1979), pp. 41-42.

12. Source unknown.

13. *Daily Meditations for Prayer* (Westchester, Ill.: Good News Publishers, 1978), p. 243.

14. Jack McAlister, *Africa at 6 A.M.* (Studio City, Calif.: World Literature Crusade, 1968), p. 11.

15. C. Peter Wagner, *Churches That Pray* (Ventura, Calif.: Regal Books, 1993), p. 184.

Chapter 14: Warfare Intimacy

1. Baker Book House, 1978.

2. A. W. Tozer, *The Pursuit of God* (Wheaton, Ill.: Tyndale House, 1982), p. 40.

3. Ibid., p. 67.

4. Ibid., p. 18.

SCRIPTURE INDEX

TOPICAL INDEX

Abhyankar, Mr., 152
Abraham, 45,57,71,99,157
accuser of our brethren, 28,143
AD 2000 and Beyond — A Handbook, 183
AD 2000 and Beyond Movement, 129-130, 136,141,181-183
Addis Ababa, 49
Adopt-a-People Clearing House, 136,183
Africa at 6 A.M., 183
Africa, African, 17,48-50,68,133-134,150-151, 181
Ahab (king), 63
Ahasuerus (king), 160-162
aiteo (Greek word for claim or demand), 94
Albania, Albanians, 17-18,21
All Heaven Waits, 31,181
All They Want Is the Truth, 183
America, American, 10,14-15,35,78,80-82, 87,105-106,137
Ammon, 55
angel, angelic, angels, 15,27-31,45-46,58-59, 62-64,72,84,100,110
Anna (prophetess), 159
Argentina, Argentine, 8,18,85,141
Argentine missions, 8,85
armor (of God), 60-61,90-91
Artaxerxes (king), 158
Asia, Asian, 39,67,98
Aycock, John, 33-39
Azariah, 178
Babylon, Babylonian, 15,39,157,177
Baker, James, III, 15
Balkans, 50
Baptist Union, Russian, 140
Barrett, David, 14
batsar (Hebrew word for inaccessible), 97
Battle Hymn of the Republic, The, 122
Baxter, J. Sidlow, 142
Beeson, Ray, 37
Berlin, 10,12-13,166,171-172
Berlin Wall, 10-12,18,20,166,168,171-172
Bible Pathway Story, The, 183
Billheimer, Paul E., 64,182
Boaz, 72-73
Bombay, 39-40,152-153
Bonnke, Reinhard, 68,182

Brainerd, David, 62
Brazil, 51
Breaking the Strongholds in Your City, 52, 182
Bright, Bill, 143
Bryant, David, 8,181
Bucharest, 13,171
Buddhism, Buddhist, Buddhists, 68,109,144
Bulgaria, Bulgarian, Bulgarians, 13,18-20, 171-172
Bush, Luis, 68,136,141,183
Calcutta, 149-150
Caleb, 70
Campus Crusade for Christ, 98,121,130, 140-141,143
Carey, William, 102-103
Ceausescu, Nicolae, 14,20
Change the World Ministries, 171
Change the World School of Prayer, 33-34, 36-38,181
Chawner, Austin, 150-151
Chile, 134
China, 17,68
Christ for the Cities, 144
Christianity Today, 131
christophany (Greek word for pre-incarnate appearance of Christ), 173
Christos (Greek word for Christ), 71
church, 4,8-9,14,16-17,21,52,64,67,70,76,82, 85-87,89,93,98,101,109,129-131,136,139, 141-144,156
Churches That Pray, 183
closure, 5,8,16-17,21,24-27,31,101,127,129, 135,137,142,179
coincidence, coincidences, 5,32,36,39,42,52, 79,126,140,163
Colombia, 144
Colorado Springs, 77-79,82,107-110,112,124, 126,181-183,191
Commonwealth of Independent States, 98,121
communism, communist, 4,8,11-13,15,19-20, 49,67,98,116,119-120,140,166,171
Communist party, 14-15,19
communist-controlled, communist-controlled nations, 10,18,98

186

For information
on Every Home for Christ's
citywide prayer and evangelism strategies
and its global vision to help reach
every home in the world
with a clear gospel message,
write:

Dick Eastman
Every Home for Christ
P. O. Box 35950
Colorado Springs, CO 80935-3595

In Canada write:

Every Home for Christ
P. O. Box 3636
Guelph, Ontario N1H 7S2
Canada

If you enjoyed *The Jericho Hour*, we would like
to recommend the following books:

Prayerwalking
by Graham Kendrick and Steve Hawthorne
This insightful book expounds on the dynamics of
advancing the cause of Christ in our neighborhoods and cities.
Authors Steve Hawthorne and Graham Kendrick
encourage systematic "prayerwalking"
and teach believers how to pray on-site
with insight for their communities.

Taking Our Cities for God
by John Dawson
This national best-seller gives you Bible-based strategies
and tactics for winning your city for God.
Author John Dawson shows you how
to discover God's purpose for your city,
discern and break spiritual strongholds,
and take the five steps to voictory.

The House of the Lord
by Francis Frangipane
In this challenging book Francis Frangipane shows believers
how to lay aside individual difficulties and doctrines
and come together in worship and warfare —
to rebuild the house of the Lord
and bring healing to their cities.

Available at your local Christian bookstore or from:

Creation House
600 Rinehart Road
Lake Mary, FL 32746
1-800-451-4598